A Documentary Novel

IN THEIR WORDS...

KATHLEEN BERGER PT, PhD

Kathleen Berger

www.accessingautism.org

Dedication

I dedicate this book to three groups. First, to my children - Kris, Chelsea and Lotus. I love you. Second, to the non speaking persons with autism, for whom supported typing opens many doors, but especially those who are still struggling to attain independence and facing closed doors.

Third, to the tireless professionals who have struggled to support their clients while at the same time enduring the criticism of their professional organizations.

Lastly, in memory of Anne Donnellan and Rosemary Crossley who fought tirelessly for nonverbal autistic people.

Prologue

Approximately 30% of children diagnosed with autism* are non or minimally able to speak words. Historically, these children were institutionalized, heavily medicated, or both. Kathleen worked with these children in the school system when her son, Kris, was born. When Kris was first diagnosed with autism and didn't speak (he only spoke two words in his life), Kathleen grieved. But then she learned about the communication strategy called Facilitated Communication Training (FCT) and Kris ended up  communicating with her with this method (See Kris' story, pg 23). It gave her great hope for his future, but they never got that chance - Kris died three months later.

Facilitated Communication is one method that falls under the umbrella of supported typing and numerous individuals with autism have become independent, even reading their words after initially using physical support of resistance or touch to their arm or hand. At the same time people with autism and their families were finding hope and success with communication, studies revealed that there could be influence when using the supports. Some professionals took this to mean there was no true communication and many professional organizations, in response to these studies, have largely stated this is a discredited technique that should not be used.

Not irrelevant here, there were instances of people being accused of child abuse by typers when using physical support. Because of the possibility for influence, this fueled the fire for detractors and the discussion turned vitriolic, including name calling, disrespect and even with one professional still using the technique reporting death threats (personal correspondence). At a recent National Institute on Deafness and Other Communication Disorders (NIDCD) web conference, with two attendees who used supported typing, one of the organizers felt the need to address social media attacks by detractors, asking for participants to be respectful and not to return to past debates: "I am personally appalled and somewhat saddened about some of what is appearing in social media related to our meeting and this sort of attack behavior will not be tolerated here." Beyond professional spheres, the debate has affected those communicating through typing leaving them frustrated at the constant question of validity and authorship.

As Kathleen had experienced clear intentional movement using the FCT technique with her son, and later many others, she never discounted that communication with supported typing was true but also acknowledged the possibility for influence. She recently submitted a paper, based on her graduate school work, on the neurology of supported typing, summarized on pg. 249 that proposes a neurologic explanation for the influence as well as other questions. Primary questions raised by these supported typing strategies include 1) How could someone learn to read without being formally taught? 2) If there is true communication coming from the typer, why is there so much influence when participating in the double blind studies? 3) How do the movement differences seen in autistic persons present and does it parallel the brain differences we see?

Kathleen uses a fiction venue to illustrate specifics with supported typing while interjecting expert opinion vignettes to address the controversies. Scientific, autobiographical and clinical reports are integrated to give the reader an understanding for things like the unique way dyspraxia presents in autism, and why both the influence *and* true communication from users makes sense.

Supported typing can be life-changing for people with autism[1] and their families. But, it is not accepted in schools or many therapy clinics and studies examining optimal implementation are limited in funding resources. Kathleen believes this is in large part to a lack of understanding and hopes this will shed some light on this poorly understood topic[1].

A NOTE ABOUT THE LAYOUT

This novel begins with a fictionalized story about supported typing. Dispersed between chapters are "Expert Opinion" vignettes where qualitative and experimental studies are integrated with autobiographical accounts and clinical observation. Links to outside information are displayed on bar codes, easily accessed on your phone vignettes. These vignettes are bracketed with this symbol: ⌐══ ₒ♡ₒ ══⌐ . Words defined on pg 239 are represented in bold.

---

[1] As there is no one size fits all approach when describing people with autism, I use people first language as well as identity first language based on the flow of the writing.

If you have a hard time switching between fiction and non fiction, feel free to read the story first and then the non fiction parts!

Table of Contents

Daisy

At 78 Daisy still got up and went to work every day. Actually, even by stamina standards of most thirty year olds, Daisy had a lot of get up and go. So much so that her husband, Tom, and she had a running joke, actually more of an understanding, where if he needed a low-key vacation day to himself all he needed to do was ask.

While Daisy's genetic make up lent to high energy, a majority of that energy was fueled by her passion for her work. It was over 40 years ago when she first met Suzie - a frail young woman in what they called a disability institute in Australia.

Daisy had been hired to provide educational services to residents. When Daisy first met Suzie, Suzie was laying on a gurney, as this was the only way the staff had figured out how to be able to move her around easily, as Daisy approached. Daisy had been told that Suzie could not talk and that she was severely retarded.

But, when their eyes met, there was a spark in Suzie's eyes that was more consistent with a thoughtful mind behind a mouth that couldn't speak words than retardation. At that moment, Daisy knew Suzie had so much to say, and Daisy knew it was her job to help her get it out. Of course, Daisy didn't know it at the time, but this would be the start to an incredible journey for both of them. Daisy would discover a way to support Suzie using a letter-board and Suzie would type her words. Several years later, Daisy would write a book, *Suzie's Coming Out* that detailed their journey.

The communication technique Daisy and Suzie used would be come to be called Facilitated Communication and later Facilitated Communication Training. While Suzie was able to demonstrate her competence in a court of law, many others who used the technique were not so lucky. In Daisy and other's excitement to share this life changing technique to others, the promoters didn't fully realize how much a typer might be influenced, especially someone with autism. And, some in the research community had done studies showing this, which, along with abuse accusations that came out using FC, led to a ridiculously vitriolic debate in the professional disability community. On one side some scientists and professionals who read the studies became convinced that the only thing that was happening was that the typers were being led by subtle or not so subtle cues.

But, to those like Suzie and Daisy who had found independent, life-changing communication with the method, there was no doubt it was a useful, much needed tool. They were firmly planted in the proponent camp of what was to be a very heated battle. Some would even receive death threats!

On this rainy, wintry Melbourne day in July, Daisy had arrived at the office by 8 am. She was in the process of evaluating several of her clients on the TONI-4, a test for non verbal intelligence that allowed for pointing to a single answer. Taking out the motor components of speaking or writing was imperative for her clients as most of these clients had been scored in what was referred to as "profound retardation" when they participated in intelligence tests that required more complex motor skills, for them to write or speak. Or, more common they were pronounced retarded by a physician with no intelligence test, based on the fact they couldn't speak words out their mouths.

Daisy had been working with her first client, Eugene, for over ten years. During that time, Eugene had written and published a poetry book and passed a 19th century history exam - among other things. But that didn't matter to those who would say that it only meant his communication partner did all those things.

Limiting his accomplishments to the only explanation they had - that all this was the result of influence by their communication partner. It didn't matter to them that that partner had not attended some of the classes and had dyslexia.

"Good morning Eugene and Sonya!" Daisy greeted Eugene and his current caregiver. Like so many folks with autism, Eugene had a hard time keeping good caregivers. Too many didn't understand the reason for some of Eugene's, as he described it, quirky behaviors. But Sonya seemed to be getting how Eugene's body and brain didn't work together. More importantly, she understood and accepted that Eugene understood everything she said - he just had a hard time getting his body and speech to respond.

"Good morning Daisy!" Sonya chimed back with Eugene waving his hands and rocking beside her.

As with most of her clients, Eugene had a special affection for Daisy. Unlike so many people who came into his life, Daisy saw Eugene as a competent, capable being. She saw beyond his autistic mannerisms and saw what Eugene named the "True me!" After so many years having teachers and therapists talk in front of him; saying things like "He can't talk" to another. Of course, there was little else that he would love to be able to do more than talk - he didn't need any reminders.

At other times when he was dysregulated and struck a table hard, or, to his horror, a person, some would tell him "Nice hands!" Other times he laughed inexplicably when someone stubbed their toe, and many teachers and staff thought his "behavior" represented what he felt inside - that he thought it was funny. It wasn't that he didn't want to be nice, or thought it was funny. It was he didn't have control over his body, and for whatever reason emotional moments triggered laughter. Eugene never fully understood this until he met Daisy. He was grateful. Daisy understood him. She saw beyond his autistic body and helped Eugene discover his true self.

"Come on Eugene! Let's show them how smart you are!" cheered Daisy, sensing Eugene was anxious. She gestured towards the therapy room.

Eugene was anxious, but also excited. He had been through so much testing in his life. So many tests filled with items he couldn't complete even though he knew the answers. If it weren't for Daisy's belief in him, he would probably be resorting more to his anxiety-relieving autistic patterns. But on this day, he rocked back and forth while slapping his hands on his legs but didn't feel the need to expand beyond those minimal patterns. He could control his emotions, to some degree, knowing that Daisy was there.

To support Eugene to the chair, Daisy touched him lightly on the shoulder. The slight touch allowed Eugene to initiate moving towards Daisy's therapy room. And, over the next 30 minutes, they sat side by side diligently working through the TONI-4.

Eugene was focused and calm, typical for when he worked on academics tasks. That's one thing the opponents of supported typing didn't have a good answer to. Why so many typers, who under typical circumstance had a tendency to be very dysregulated - to jump or pace or flap their hands, would sit for an hour focused and calm when they were engaged in a cognitive task that involved typing.

Not surprisingly, Eugene did well - he only got one out of 60 wrong. When he was finished and Daisy told him the score, Eugene visibly relaxed and they talked about the test. Funnily, Eugene got a little stuck on the question he got wrong. Turns out the question asked if a block was to the right or left of the triangle and Eugene got it mixed up. Which made sense, Eugene often had difficulty with directional cues unless he was clued in by the context and he had no context to navigate.

"What else do you want to tell me?" Daisy asked as she retrieved an IPAD from her bookshelf and opened up the communication APP. She then squeezed Eugene's elbow and he moved his fingers to the letters and typed, "THAT WAS EASY!"

Seven more client sessions later with a lunch break squeezed in and Daisy was ready to go home. Tom, was her rock. Suzie had come to live with them eventually, and they had many happy years as a family before Suzie died at thirty-seven. So, it was just she and Tom now.

Tom was a great cook and he delighted at treating visiting American friends to his famous kangaroo curry. Or, at least famous to his family and friends! It was more famous for the reaction he got than how awesome the curry was. Daisy wasn't sure what he was planning for dinner, but she looked forward to it nonetheless. Tom kept her grounded and Daisy loved their quiet evenings together, even if she sandwiched it between answering the many emails she received, and answered, sometimes late into the night.

As she did every afternoon, Daisy checked the metro schedule. Never mind that she had taken the metro for more than 30 years, facts like when the trains run never seemed to manage to stick in her brain, something she attributed to her ADHD. Well, she had never been officially diagnosed, never really saw the point as she liked her life and seemed to be doing well enough, so why rock the boat?

Beyond enjoying a partner who liked to cook, one of the many reasons Daisy was grateful for Tom was his patience and humility as a steadfast, patient partner who often waited behind the scenes as Daisy was stopped by yet another participant at a conference needing support or as Daisy dashed off to respond to a recent email from a family. Daisy rarely said no, always lending an encouraging word and hope to parents looking for support on communication strategies. Strategies that might be the only reason their child could communicate with them - their avenue to the world. Tom was always there by her side, and Daisy knew that without his support, she would have a lot less space to hold her clients. Remembering Tom waiting at home, Daisy grabbed her bag and rushed out the door.

She would have to run if she was going to catch the 6:10 train, but then she pretty much would have to run any time she was catching the train; at any given moment Daisy had at least ten things on her plate at a time; had a tendency to distraction; and was consistently running late. Beyond that, Daisy didn't waste time. Ever since, maybe even before, she met Suzie, Daisy had a passion for providing opportunities to people like Eugene, who had been marginalized by how society understood them and Daisy had a way to "unmarginalize" them and she wasn't going to waste any time.

Daisy grabbed some files and an article she wanted to read that one of the parents had shared with her on a new typing technique called "Spelling to Communicate", or S2C for short. Daisy stuffed the files and article into her shoulder bag and, with coat unzipped, headed out the door toward the metro stop.

Daisy didn't even like to stop long enough to do things like zip up her jacket.

He leaned against a pole under the cover of the metro platform. The pandemic had made things easier for him to disguise himself - especially in the winter. He just had to throw on a mask and don the hood of his sweatshirt. He would throw the sweatshirt away when he was done.

He had never met Daisy but he wasn't worried about recognizing her as he had seen a couple of pictures and the crowd at the Metro station was thin. The job shouldn't be too difficult. Just a quick shove and then escape quickly to a car that was parked below the platform. He had taken off the plates and left it there earlier in the day.

Daisy arrived on the platform with a minute to spare. At first he didn't recognize her, but just as he heard the train in the distance, she turned her head and he recognized her profile.

Daisy stood maybe ten feet away and he took a couple steps towards her. In just a moment, the train would be close and he would shove her onto the tracks. Job accomplished and he would get his payment.

Daisy noticed someone approaching out of the corner of her eye, a chill started up her spine. "Don't be ridiculous." she told herself, but still felt uneasy. Glancing down, she noticed her shoelace was untied.

He saw her glance over at him but he wasn't worried. There's no way she knew what he was there for - that he was planning on throwing her onto the tracks. Save some crime bosses, most people didn't walk around thinking someone was going to murder them. Especially someone like Daisy, whom most everyone loved.

The train approached and his body tensed in anticipation.

Just at that moment Daisy leaned over to tie her shoes. The man felt nothing but the wind from the train as he lurched forward to push Daisy. He missed and fell onto the tracks just before the train arrived. Oblivious to his intentions. Daisy stood horrified as she heard his screams.

She had no clue that in a weird way her ADHD brain had just saved her life.

Noreen

Noreen. He had been following her around for the last couple of weeks to evaluate her comings and goings and the best way to do it. Do what you might ask? Succinctly, he had been hired to kill her and make it look like an accident. It wasn't his usual type of work. Usually he was a soldier for a crime group in Chicago, but when his boss asked him to take the job, he couldn't say no.

It wasn't until the second week of following Noreen around that he began to formulate a plan. Every Tuesday Noreen drove up to Big Bear, a mountain town in the San Bernadino mountains. Noreen stopped at a group home for persons with autism and spent a couple of hours to support the residents in their communication.

Noreen had been a speech therapist for over 30 years and her work passion was centered around supported typing with people with autism. Similar to Daisy, one of Noreen's first clients, Sherri, wanted to try a new typing strategy, one that they had heard about through Daisy. Through her journey of supporting Sherri and Sherri becoming independent, even graduating college, Noreen learned a ton and also learned that this could help hundreds, if not thousands, of children in a way that no other treatment she encountered in all her years of experience could. Plus, Noreen was a gregarious soul and she truly loved her time with her clients.

At Sherri's request, Noreen first learned about facilitated communication, the kind of supported typing she started out with, when she attended a one day continuing education course. That was the first she had learned of Daisy, whom she would eventually become dear friends with through presentations at many other conferences.

It was a simple technique, really. You put your hand out to offer support to a client, and you then give resistance to the arm or hand so they could then move forward to select a letter on a keyboard, tablet or laminated letterboard. Noreen thought back to one of the first kiddos she typed with, Adam. She was lucky that Adam was fairly well regulated. It was a great learning experience for her, as she had learned over the years just how dysregulated folks could get. One particular session at a retreat a client had an episode and she ended up getting body checked in a bathroom. Later that same client successfully dislodged the toilet from it's mooring to the wall.

With Adam though, on her first day supporting someone typing, she felt the intentionality of his forward movement. It was very clear. He had filled in some blanks and answered "Doug" for the therapy dog he had met that day, and "Fouve" for how old he was. Though neither word was spelled correctly that day, Noreen knew it was Adam spelling the word as there was a clear intention and force when Adam pushed against resistance. She didn't understand why so many of the detractors didn't at least try it. Once you felt the quality and intensity of the movement, there was no going back. Maybe that was why they didn't seek it out? In a lot of ways, professionally, she took a lot of heat for continuing to support facilitated communication, including being shunned by some old colleagues. Noreen imagined other therapists might be scared to try supported typing for fear of the pushback they might get.

While Noreen's first account of typing with Adam was fairly unremarkable, it was Adam's mom's story of when they first typed that Noreen liked to share. It related to some of the controversy questions and it was also a great example for parents starting out in their typing journey to just stick with it, as well as a good illustration of how to give the supports and assume competence. A week after Noreen's first experience with Adam, Adam's family went to visit his grandmother. Adam's dad was downstairs with the kids when Kate heard Adam getting upset. Her husband told her, "I have no idea what's going on.

We were just watching videos and he just started screaming." Kate went through all of Adam's favorite things - Jon Mitchell, Adam particularly loved LADIES OF THE CANYON; a bath and a favorite blanket. But all that happened was Adam seemed to get more and more angry. It was weird. So often before he had started typing Adam's cries would come out kind of vague. But since he had typed with Noreen, the tone to his cries had changed. It was as if he realized that he could communicate - he had found his voice.

For several minutes Kate and Adam worked through his favorites and Adam's tone was very clearly one of anger, and getting stronger. Kate eventually got out the canon communicator device they had bought off of ebay, a device that printed out on a short piece of paper what was typed. As soon as she had settled Adam in front of her with the canon communicator, he had calmed down. Silence. Then when she offered her hand as Noreen had shown her, Adam took her hand and very clearly typed "RAFFI", one of Adam's favorite music videos. And, after talking to Adam's dad later, the one that she found out had been playing before Adam's dad switched it out for the "Old McDonald" video his sister was requesting. Adam had been sitting in the corner playing with a toy, seeming to not pay attention to what was on the TV. As Raffi was almost over, Joe switched them out. Apparently Adam had been paying attention!

This was so huge for Kate as for the first several years of Adam's life, she worried unceasingly about what his future would hold. As a physical therapist, she had worked in special education. She had worked with teenagers who were so drugged due to what is referred to as self-injurious behaviors that they pretty much slept on and off throughout the day, sometimes drooling from the side effects of the medications as their heads rested on their desk, or on the floor. She did not want this for Adam. She did not want this for anyone.

So, the fact that Adam had communicated with her, with a word, and the fact that it was so clear what his communication was and his motor intent with his pointing was clear, for the first time in five years, gave her hope. A lot of hope.

Before Adam typed with her, she had misgivings about using the method as she had heard cautionary tales of a "ouiji board" type phenomenon. But after experiencing it first hand, she was convinced that this could be a life-changing tool for Adam and was all-in. Actually, Kate made Noreen a little crazy at times as she always wanted to get into a detailed discussion of neurology and the "why" behind the supported typing.

But Noreen never tired of hearing these kind of stories. It's why she does what she does. What could be better than helping a child communicate with a parent - especially when that parent thought, had been told, that their child would probably never talk to them. Many had been told their child was severely and profoundly retarded, some even before their child had ever taken an IQ test.

But like most professionals and parents who interacted with these autistic souls, most parents sensed a unique intelligence that they couldn't quite define. They couldn't quite define it - it was the way the kids looked at you or laughed unexpectedly at a joke that was fairly complex. Not a joke, but she remembered Adam's mom sharing with her how Adam hysterically belly- laughed when they went to see the puffin exhibit at Sea world. Grandma had been visiting and Kate and her mom traded off going into the exhibit while the other waited out with Adam's sleeping baby and toddler sisters. She remembered Kate telling her it wasn't so much to see the exhibit as it was to enjoy Adam's laugh at the silly looking creatures flying underwater.

Noreen thought of Adam and his family and smiled. In almost every way, she felt so privileged to be able to support Adam and his communication. How could you not get joy from your work? Well, there was always Glen Donovan. Donovan was a therapist she was friends with early in her career, and had even gone on a date once. But early on in the supported typing "movement", they found themselves squarely on opposite sides. There were some professionals who would do pretty much anything to stop her from supporting her families and Glen Donovan was one of those. She didn't get it fully, but it was true.

Expert Opinion

The Early Days. The Beginnings Of Supported Typing And Considering Motor Difficulties In Autism.

Rosemary Crossley met Annie MacDonald when she was hired as a play leader at St Nicholas Hospital in Melbourne, Australia for severely handicapped children in the mid 1970s. Rosemary noticed Annie seemed to be much more aware than a diagnosis of severe and profound retardation would warrant. With Rosemary's support, Annie would eventually be able to hit letters on a board to communicate, even passing a message unknown to Rosemary to verify her communication at the Supreme Court Of Victoria.

Annie had severe cerebral palsy, but Rosemary would go on to try the communication strategy, come to be known as Facilitated Communication Training, or FCT, with other diagnoses such as Down syndrome and autism. She found it to be successful for many of her clients and began sharing it with others.

Douglas Biklen, an education professor at Syracuse University in Syracuse, New York, learned of Rosemary's work and, after a visit to meet Rosemary, details his observations of clients in a 1990 article in the *Harvard Educational Review, Communication Unbound: Autism and Praxis* and then in a 1993 book, *Communication Unbound: How Facilitated Communication is challenging traditional views of Autism and Ability/Disability*:

> Jonothan Solaris cannot speak. David Armbruster can say few words, usually unintelligible. Both are young adolescents classified as autistics... I was not surprised by how either of them appeared. Theirs were the behaviors of autism. But what I did not anticipate was that their communication with me would assault my assumptions about autism and ultimately yield important lessons for education.

> ... when Crossley asked if they had anything to tell me, Jonothan began to type on a Canon communicator (a small typing device with a dot-matrix tape output.). With a staff member's hand on his shoulder, Jonothan typed, ILIKEDOUGBUT_HHEISMAAD. Seeing what Jonothan had written, Corssley asked why he thought he was "mad", whereupon he typed, HETALKSTOMELIKEIMHUMAN. By MAAD he had meant "crazy".

In Biklen's original paper, *Communication Unbound: Autism and Praxis*, he proposes that the communication difficulties seen in autism can be seen as one of a disorder of praxis, not cognition. He explains that he uses the term praxis in a general rather than technical or scientific way to describe "the problem people with autism have in speaking or enacting their words or ideas."

Now I am not sure if Biklen was aware how complicated the study of praxis problems was/is, but it would be the subject of heated debate for the next few decades. I mention it here as I want to point out that Biklen proposed that praxis difficulties *may* lay behind what typing supporters were seeing, but only in the general sense. This was back in the early 90s.

The recent dyspraxia studies were not done until the late 2000s. I am not sure detractors such as Lilienfield, citation below, who have criticized praxis theories, understand these studies and how praxis presents in autism. For example, Lilienfeld says in the below paper, "FC is premised on the notion that autistic children suffer not from an intellectual and affective impairment but from an exclusively motor impairment termed developmental apraxia, which impedes their ability to speak properly." But, recent developmental dyspraxia/apraxia studies look more at the ability to perform pretend gestures such as pretending to brush one's hair, which include control of volitional movement of the arms and hands. And, when Biklen proposes praxis may underlie the challenges typers face, he describes it as "the problem people with autism have in speaking or enacting their words or ideas." - not simply the inability to speak. It is the inability to enact thoughts or ideas that impedes the access to a keyboard. Now, you might think Lilienfield's confusion is due to the fact his paper was written before many of the recent dyspraxia studies, but he makes a similar statement in a talk he gave just 8 years ago, years after those studies came out. Of course, I spent a good 10 years to have a solid grasp on dyspraxia and I am nowhere near knowing all there is on the subject.

Lilienfeld SO. Scientifically unsupported and supported interventions for childhood psychopathology: a summary. Pediatrics. 2005 Mar;115(3):761-4. doi: 10.1542/peds.2004-1713. PMID: 15741383.

We will discuss in more detail what praxis/dyspraxia is later in this book, but you can think of praxis as the ability to understand and learn *meaningful* gestures. There have been several studies in the last 10-20 years showing praxis is affected in autistic persons. But, in the early 90s there was heated debate as to whether motor difficulties had anything to do with autism which continues to this day.

Surprisingly, or maybe not surprisingly, in Kanner's 1943 paper, one of the first to describe autism, there is evidence of difficulties in understanding and/or producing meaningful movements or gestures. At 4 months of age, when a typical baby's parent walks in a room, the baby adjusts their posture:

> According to Gesell, the average child at 4 months of age makes an anticipatory motor adjustment by facial tension and shrugging attitude of the shoulders when lifted from a table or placed on a table. Gesell commented:

> This universal experience is supplied by the frequency with which an infant is picked up by his mother and other persons. It is therefore highly significant that almost all mothers of our patients recalled their astonishment at the children's failure to assume at any time an anticipatory posture prepatory to being picked up. One father recalled that his daughter (Barbara) did not for years change her physiognomy

or position in the least when the parents, upon coming home after a few hours' absence, approached her crib talking to her and making ready to pick her up.

Though Kanner's original 1943 paper describing autism includes evidence of dyspraxia; studies as early as 1977 indicated that imitation (a part of the praxis system) was affected; and Biklen proposed general praxis difficulties, research looking into motor differences at all, much less praxis difficulties in autism was sparse until the early 2000s. One paper cited frequently in the early years of the supported typing community was a 1981 article done by Vilensky, Damasio and Maurer where they suggest gait of autistic individuals were similar to gait of person's who had Parkinson's disease. I would eventually come to study under a colleague of Ralph Mauer, one of the authors on this paper.

To illustrate the motor debate, Bernard Rimland, a famous psychologist, a strong autism advocate and father of a child with autism wrote:

> It has been widely recognized for many decades that the vast majority of autistic persons are quite unimpaired with regard to their finger dexterity and gross motor capabilities. They have in fact often been described as especially dexterous and coordinated. The literature abounds with stories of young autistic children who can take apart and reassemble small mechanical devices, build towers of blocks and dominos higher than a normal adult can, assemble jigsaw puzzles and climb to dangerously high places without falling. The files of the Autism Research

Institute contain over 17,000 questionnaires completed by the parents of autistic children. Finger dexterity is one question we've asked about since 1965. Most parents indicate that their children are average or above in the use of their hands. The idea that autism is, or typically involves, a "movement disorder" is simply ludicrous.

Early Observations On Touch Cues And Movement Intentionality

Early in the 1990s, this author, a physical therapist, realized if she touched her son's hand with a light touch it felt like he would move intentionally to a toy and knew his colors and alphabet. Years later I was surprised to find a passage from Biklen's first book, *Communication Unbound*, describing one of his first observations with Rosie and a 24 year old man, Louis. It was surprisingly similar to my first 'facilitation' experience with Kris:

She began the session by asking him to press down

on various pictures or letters and that announces the user's choice, for example, "Right, that's the apple."

As Crossley asked the questions, tears began to roll down Louis's face. He was crying silently. She reassured him, telling him that she would do it with him. She held her hand on top of Louis's right arm. In response to the command, "Press the red car," Louis put his index finger on it and Crossley helped him to push down. Louis was moving slowly. He seemed tentative. The machine instructed him to find the circle, which he did. He followed with correct answers to square, triangle, circle and triangle. He hit them all, five of five.

Similar to the intentional movement felt by Rosie and Kathy, Ido Kedar's mom, Tracey, shares on a video that she first learned her son recognized letters was when they were doing birthday party  invitations and she had to put her hand on Ido's hand, supporting him to write, and felt him moving intentionally (at :46. Ido and his mom would eventually write a book.

In India, around this time, Soma Mukhopadhyay was working with her son, Tito, to type on a keyboard. When a doctor told her that she was influencing what was being typed, she taught Tito how to write, initially starting by securing a pencil to his hand with a rubber band. Soma would go on to start the **Rapid Prompting Method** (RPM to support learning and communication in persons with autism who were limited in communication. Soma has a rhythmic energy when she works with the kids, repeating phrases like "That's it." "Keep going!" in a rhythmic way. I have since worked with music therapists who study rhythm and how it can support movement. I think Soma has tapped into this. Later, more on Soma and Tito.

In 1992 Dov Shestack was born. A couple years later he would be diagnosed with autism and his parents, Jon And Portia Shestack, would start Cure Autism Now, or CAN, to fund autism research. CAN would later evolve into Autism Speaks, a national organization that funds autism research. Portia would learn of Soma and Tito and Tito's writing at a scientific conference and would bring them to Los Angeles where Soma would work with Dov, who began to be able to communicate through typing.

Portia also organized a visit for Tito to see Michael Merzenich, a famous neuroscientist at the University of California San Francisco, and they would collaborate on a scientific paper. In 2006 the book *Strange Sons: Two mothers, two sons, and a quest to unlock the hidden world of autism* was published. Portia wrote the book detailing their experience.

Merzenich, M., Bonneh, Y., Belmonte, M., Pei, F., Iversen P., Kenet T., Akshoomoff N., Adini Y., Simon H., Moore I., Houde J. (2008) Cross-Modal Extinction In A Boy With Severely Autistic Behaviour and High Verbal Intelligence. Cognitive Neuropsychology, (25)5, 635-652. https:// doi.org/10.1080/02643290802106415

My First Experience With FC - Kris' Story

In my first year as a therapist one of my clients was a six- year-old little boy, Max, with a diagnosis of developmental delay. He had no expressive language but had made up his own signs for yes and no. Max could read at the 6th grade reading level following along with his hand (with no one touching his hand.) It was hard to know exactly what he understood - and I moved into a different job before I was able to learn more about him, but he definitely could read the word 'definitely'. His favorite show was Wheel of Fortune.

That was 5 years before my son, Kris, was born. When Kris was 6 months old I took him out of the bath one night and his body began to jerk in what I would learn was a cluster of seizures called infantile spasms. Kris' seizures caused delays that presented in a way that the doctors' called 'autistic like' challenges. Kris was very active physically, non-verbal, and I had been told by a doctor that he was severely mentally retarded.

Our lives were filled with an obsession over what had caused Kris' seizures and what we could do to stop them. We tried many medications, some less traditional avenues (such as allergies to foods) and two brain surgeries. None of these treatments were able to stop Kris' seizures.

Kris' favorite activities were listening to Joni Mitchell, watching Wheel of Fortune and watching Disney sing along videos and Raffi concert tapes . When Kris was between the age of 2 or 3 I bought a 'Touch and Tell' toy (what was then fairly high tech where the machine asked you: 'Where is the blue circle?', etc.) As I worked with Kris on this he would reach for my hand to go through the motions. As a physical therapist I was practiced in the art of facilitation – where a therapist helps or guides a person to do a movement, letting them take over when they can.

The facilitation of FC is not the facilitation OTs and PTs talk about with NDT (Neurodevelopmental Therapy) and movement facilitation - maybe somewhat of where the confusion comes from. With FC the facilitator actually resists the movement, or "amplifies" the proprioceptive sense. With the facilitation in NDT, therapists are trained in facilitating movement where you *do* guide the client. One notable observation with this was that this was an activity that Kris seemed to enjoy and would attend to for longer periods than other activities I tried to encourage him to do. There were very few things he would sit down and attend to for very long.

As I worked with Kris on the Touch and Tell he seemed to know his colors and the parts of the house, a dog vs. cat etc. But, his movement was VERY tentative. So tentative that I barely mentioned it to Will (Kris' Dad, my husband) and didn't discuss it with anyone else. Kris had been diagnosed as being severely retarded by a reputable child neurologist, and I wasn't really sure what was happening. Was I guiding his hand? It didn't feel like that. It felt like he was moving, and he would sit and attend to it, which was unusual. In fact, when we were in the hospital for a surgery evaluation, my mom tried the touch and tell like she had seen me do with Kris. Here eyes widened, feeling Kris' movement, and she looked at me, "He knows his colors!"

Another important aspect to consider was the many days we spent encouraging Kris to sign. He had his favorite songs and we made up different signs to go with them. We encouraged Kris to 'ask' for them. If we pushed Kris in the swing we stopped his swing and encouraged him to ask for more (in sign). He would reach for our hands to 'help' him. Knowing what it was we were asking, but unable to make his body do it.

All of these things played through my mind as I read about facilitated communication. Max, the commonality between he and Kris watching Wheel of Fortune; Kris watching the sing along videos with the bouncing ball, his reaching for our hands to help him. It was possible that he'd taught himself some. And, he certainly seemed to be stuck somewhere motorically.

When I filled out the application to attend Adam's Camp I asked that someone try facilitated communication with him, as I had just become aware of the technique. There were two speech therapists there. One who had used FC and found success, and the other who was not convinced.

The second day after therapy at Adam's Camp, Sari, the FC speech therapist touched bases with me as I picked up Kris. She said he had typed 'fouve' for how old he was (he had just turned five) and 'doug' for the therapy dog that was there that day.

We decided that if there was even the remotest possibility of Kris being capable, we had to pursue it. It certainly wasn't a 'miracle breakthrough'. Kris had no interest in typing with us at camp. He would push the board away and cry. I can only imagine it was pretty scary for him, or he just was so unused to it. We had always communicated with him using our words, never really knowing how much he understood. He had always communicated with us by leading us to things or crying. To make that jump with us must have seemed pretty strange. For skeptics, their interpretation might be that he was limited in what he wanted to say, or that this was all a big hoax.

When we left Adam's camp, we drove to visit my mother-in- law for a couple of days. I had ordered a couple of new overlays, including an ABC one, for the Touch and Tell but hadn't had a chance to use them before we left for Adam's Camp. When Will got up with Kris the next morning he got them out and tried them with Kris. His first, hushed as Kris was in the room, words to me later were, "He knows his ABC's! I mean he got a little mixed up between upper and lower case, but he knows his ABC's!" Relevant to this story is that Will is a man who has a Ph.D. in Political Science and is firmly rooted in the 'numbers crunching' section of that field. He needs to see facts and the scientific studies to prove it. Or, he needs to experience it first hand. That morning with Kris he experienced who was doing the typing and who was not. And, Kris showed him he knew his ABC's.

Of course, though I was certainly less skeptical than Will to begin with, I had yet to have Kris try and communicate anything with me. It was all so strange. How could this possibly be?

Later that day I was upstairs and I heard Kris start crying downstairs. Will was down there with the three kids. As I walked down the stairs and looked at Will quizzically he said, "I have no idea. He was just sitting in the corner and got upset."

Kris was really upset so I brought him upstairs and started trying his different 'favorites' - blanky, music, bath. Kris kept crying and was getting more upset. After several minutes I decided to get out the letter board given to us at camp. He had been crying rather loudly for the last 10 minutes or more. As soon as we sat down with the letter board he was quiet. I took his hand and gave resistance in a motion away from the board, like Sukhi had showed me. He stuck his finger out and with a lot of resistance and clear movement on his part, typed out Raffi.

I asked him if he wanted to watch Raffi and he pointed to the word yes. Thankfully Will's mom had two VCRs and I took him upstairs and popped in the Raffi tape he liked to watch. He was happy and quiet as a clam.

Glen Donovan

Glen sat behind the desk in the office he kept at one of the **Applied Behavior Analysis** clinics for kids with autism.

"What?! How could anyone be so stupid?" Glen barked into the phone, prompted by being told that Daisy's assassination did not happen. "I guess I will have to look elsewhere for someone who is actually competent."

Glen wasn't always so antagonistic towards the supported typing technique, but as events unfolded, he became more and more frustrated that this was still going on. Not only going on, but going on strong. At first, as a behavior therapist working with individuals with complex communication needs, many who had autism, he was curious and hopeful to learn more. But then, there came reports of abuse using a technique where someone was holding your hand. And, there were studies now showing that that same touch allowed for influence. Who could think this was anything more than another snake oil? Who could think this was real?

Of course, it didn't help that one of those accused was his brother. At Glen's prompting, his nephew. Jay, had been placed at a residential facility that tried facilitated communication when it first came out. It was Jay's case, along with a handful of others, that prompted Glen and some colleagues to test, and then protest the technique.

Though in the recesses of his mind he could imagine his brother, Dwayne, doing just what his nephew accused him of - hitting him to the point of causing bruises - this was exactly what their father did to them growing up. While Dwayne got married and had children, Glen never had children and had stuffed all that behind his professional persona.

There was no way he was going to let his brother be labeled a child abuser. No flipping way. Glen and Dwayne were like so many who had been accused of child abuse, and denied it - they had no problem with lying. It probably came down to their narcissism, narcissism that came, at least partially, from their own childhood abuse.

It was like their hearts never were able to grow enough to feel true empathy for others. For Glen, it was as if he was the Grinch in reverse. The more stories came out declaring how successful some individuals were; the more supported typing techniques and stories were shared in the media it was as if his heart grew smaller and smaller each time - until he reached the breaking point and all bets were off. He reasoned to others that it was to protect the children. He reasoned to himself that anything was ok to protect the children, and, at least in *his* mind, it was reasonable to resort to hiring hit men. He had tried everything else and they wouldn't shut up, so this was their deserved punishment, or at least he thought this in the recesses of his mind. He thought by killing off all the major figures in supported typing, he could finally end this saga.

Perhaps not surprisingly, Glen had been one of the main proponents when the Judge Rotenberg Educational Center began using electric shock treatments to control behavior of many of their residents with autism in the early 1970s. A horrifying concept for most people with a heart, Glen happily jumped on the bandwagon when a colleague approached him.

Glen was all about control and power, and the visual of a difficult child getting shocked secretly gave him a thrill.

So, it was not surprising that Glen found himself sitting at his desk discussing finding a competent hit man with a member of the Mob. He had found him on the dark web - who knew you could google how to hire a hit man. Glen hung up the phone and began sorting through the center's budget. He needed to figure out how to come up with more money.

Jake And Meg

She wasn't sure if she had done the right thing. Or not. She'd heard negative things about what most people in the autism world referred to as ABA - Applied Behavior Analysis. But then she'd also heard encouraging stories. They'd been at the center for two months and the jury was out as to how much it had helped her son, Jake.

As a single mom, Meg had limited resources so she had approached the center to see if she could possibly get a scholarship, and they had worked out a deal where she came by three times a week after work and cleaned the center. It didn't take too long, and she could bring Jake with her.

Tonight he was playing with one of those "See and Say" toys where you pull the lever and an arrow points to animal and makes the animal's sound. She wasn't sure why Jake was so drawn to this particular toy, but he was. Maybe it was because it was one of the few toys he could make work?

Jake had what folks called "non-verbal autism". Jake was a typical healthy baby as far as anyone knew, but at 6 months of age he started having seizures that affected his development. Or, at least that's what the pediatric neurologist had told her. It seemed no one really knew what causes autism. Probably different things, but for Jake she attributed it to the way the seizures affected his brain.

Jake didn't sit still for very long. At home, Meg kept some side tables bare as for some reason Jake liked to stand up when he was watching some of his favorite shows, mainly

Wheel of Fortune and some sing-along-videos - the ones with the bouncing balls over the words.

Autism was such a funny thing. What she had known about autism before Jake's brith you could fit in a thimble, or whatever that expression was. Her impression was that autism meant you didn't want to be around other people - you weren't interested in relationships.

Yet, Jake showed her that he *did* want relationships in the ways he could. Like the day she came home from the hospital from a minor health procedure and a friend had been watching Jake. She remembered walking in and sitting next to the table he was sitting on top of, and talking to her friend. Though Jake had no way of saying, "Hi Mom! Welcome home! I missed you!" he could express it in different ways. On this day, he scootched over to the edge of the table and patted her gently on the top of her head. He didn't have to say it. She knew what it meant.

Meg wondered again about why it was that Jake had such a hard time playing with most toys. She thought about the apraxia or dyspraxia other parents and professionals talked about. It seemed crazy that even though Jake could walk and do things like push the See and Say lever, for some reason he had a hard time controlling his movement. Of course, he didn't do things like typical babies did like imitate you pouring water out of a cup in the bathtub, or make his hands do the made-up-signs for songs Jake liked her to sing to him when he was taking a bath.

Meg glanced over at Jake, felt the familiar pang in her heart of love mixed with worry, and thought about the "refrigerator mother" syndrome that mothers of children with autism had endured in the 50s and 60s. She had seen a documentary on PBS about it. There was a Freudian psychologist, Bruno Bettelheim, who came up with a theory that autism was caused by a mother's lack of affection. He suggested that the treatment was a "parentectomy" - that the children be removed from their home and placed in institutions. In these institutions then they would take all the toys away and isolate them. She couldn't remember in this moment the reasoning behind this. If these kids were affected so strongly by what these psychologists described as an inability to bond with a cold mother, why would it make sense to isolate them?

She came across a paper talking about how the impact of the refrigerator mother syndrome theory hung on culturally long after the theory was debunked in the mid 1960s. She remembered when the doctor told her Jake was autistic. It wasn't that she wasn't expecting it, it was that gut feeling that somehow that diagnosis meant she had messed up as a mother. It wasn't a rationale thought. She knew how much she loved Jake. She knew he felt that. She didn't even know where that guilty feeling came from. For a long time she just thought it must be the feeling any parent would have if they received a major diagnosis - kind of like the stages of grief. Only in this case the first stage was self-blame.

But after she learned more about the refrigerator mother syndrome, she wondered how much of that came from a sort of societal hangover from the predominant autism theory in the mid 20th century. After all, if there is a theory that most so- called experts agreed was the cause of a disorder, it would make sense that it doesn't automatically go away when one scientist writes a paper disagreeing with it. Or maybe the notion that mothers caused autism just hung on as there was no real answer as to what *really* caused autism.

It didn't matter really. She was just glad she lived in this time, not the 1950s. Meg glanced over at Jake again and tried to fathom how hard it must have been for mothers of children with autism at that time. How horrible it must have felt to be blamed for the autism, and then to have the solution be to hand over your child to an institution as they "knew better".

Meg and Jake had an appointment the following day to see a new speech therapist, Noreen. Meg had learned of a typing communication strategy for kids with autism that had difficulty talking, Supported Typing, from another mom whose child had started using it.

Meg and Jake had started attending a social group. In theory, it was for the kids, but in reality it was just as much, if not more, a support group for the moms. Her friend, Suzy, had been gushing about how her son, Ben, had spelled answers to a short paragraph that had been read to him.

Meg had heard about the typing strategies, but had been steered away by other professionals when she brought it up. She was told the American Speech Hearing and Language Association and the American Pediatric Association cautioned against trying it, saying it was discredited and could be dangerous. So Meg had called an old speech therapist friend who, as it turns out, had just run into an old client who was independent and read his words as or after he typed them.

Meg's friend had discharged him from therapy as he wasn't making progress, but was now second guessing herself - big time..

Though her friend recounted the cautions Noreen had heard, she also said she couldn't explain how this non verbal child with autism could have learned to communicate so richly. When she had worked with this boy, he could get aggressive and had bite marks on his hands from constantly biting them. The most they were able to accomplish after two years of work was two simple request on what was called a PECS board - picture exchange communication system, but then Ben ended up getting stuck on these and would just request a coke. Her friend planned on taking a course to learn more as soon as she could. That sealed the deal and Meg called and scheduled an appointment the next day.

Jake's vocalizations brought her back to the present. It was time to finish up and get home.

Jake And Noreen

When Noreen greeted them in the waiting room, Meg instantly liked her. She had a no-nonsense manner about her countered by an equally warm, respectful manner as she greeted Jake.

"Hey Jake! Nice to meet you. Let's head back to my room and we can see what you have to say." Noreen spoke confidently. It surprised Meg that she spoke to Jake first, and like she knew he understood what she said. Of all the professionals Meg had dealt with since Jake's diagnosis, Noreen seemed to know that Jake was "in there".

Jake's hands moved from a"high-guard" position when Noreen first approached to a relaxed position down at his side. Jake obviously relaxed in her presence. You could tell from his posture, but also in that he stood up and followed Noreen without a prompt or holding a hand.

Once they were seated in Noreen's room, Noreen brought out a letterboard - a laminated piece of paper with letters on it similar to the keys on a computer. There were also a couple of small white boards and dry erase markers laid in front of them.

"Jake, there's a woman who lives in Australia, Daisy Fudge, who found that when she gave physical support to people who she knew with cerebral palsy or autism who had difficulty speaking words, and then provided them with access to letters, they were able to show that they could type words. She found out that even though they had been considered intellectually disabled, they were so much smarter than people had thought. We don't really understand why it works. We just know it does work."

Noreen picked up one of the white boards and a marker. "What I am going to do is to write some words down on the board. I will say them as I write them in case you are unfamiliar with a word, and then I'll follow up with some questions."

Noreen paused for a moment and looked at Jake. "It's not about quizzing you because I know you are really smart. It's more about getting you to feel comfortable with the movement to the letters. To have you get a chance to get comfortable with me, and show me how much support you need."

As Noreen spoke, Jake sat still and calm. It was remarkable to Meg - Jake never sat that still. "Wow!" Jake thought, dismayed. "She knows about the words that float around in my head!"

Noreen wrote and spoke four words on the white board. "Four. Five. Three. One." Then she wrote a nonsense word, "Gobbledygook." She placed the board in front of Jake. "Jake, I want you to take a few seconds, look at the choices and think about your answer." Noreen flipped the white board over so Jake couldn't see the words and asked, "How old are you, Jake?"

Noreen then flipped the board over and said," take a minute to think about your answer." Then she reached down and held out her hand, offering it to Jake. Jake put his hand in hers and Meg saw Noreen squeeze his hand and push back, bending Jake's elbow.

Jake looked right at the white board and Meg saw him reach forward and touch the word "five". "Huh", she thought, "Well, Jake is five, but then Noreen knew that. Was he reaching or was she guiding? If she was guiding, why was it that Jake was sitting so calmly ?" Meg tried to think back on a time when Jake sat so calmly without being in a moving car. She couldn't.

"Great!" Noreen praised. "Let's move on to another question. "Ok Jake. what is your favorite food?" Six choices were written this time on the white board: French fries, broccoli, celery, crackers, something else and more than one. Again she offered her hand to Jake and gave it a squeeze when he placed his hand in hers.

Noreen turned over the board again quickly and flipped it back so Jake could see, "Give it a second and think about your answer and then make your choice."

Meg watched Jake stare intently at the board then reach forward with his hand. Meg knew what she thought Jake would choose, but was surprised when Jake chose the "more than one" choice.

Noreen erased the more than one choice on the board and they went through the hand offering followed by a squeeze and wait routine. This time Jake was quick to pick French fries and then broccoli. Such a simple question, and yet so huge. There was no way that Noreen would think that broccoli was one of Jake's favorite foods. Meg's eyes brimmed and a couple of silent tears slid down her face.

In that moment, Meg knew it was Jake communicating. In that same moment, she saw the world open up for him in a way she had cautioned herself not to dream about since his diagnosis. This was huge.

What Now?

Meg had serious misgivings the following day as she drove Jake to the center. Noreen had told her about the idea of presuming competence. Really such a simple idea, it meant that you should assume your child is aware and able to understand even though they may not show this to you in a way that you are able to recognize or understand. According to Noreen, Jake's dyspraxia made it so that he was stuck in a body that could do things like walking and eating, or do an over-learned movement, but often wouldn't cooperate when it was a thinking, more complex task. Essentially, he was stuck in a body that wouldn't do what he wanted it to do.

Noreen simplified it, "You can think of it as being stuck in a body that has difficulty starting, stopping or sustaining a movement."

She illustrated with an example, "Say you're in a day-long class and you have the urge to go the bathroom. You look at the clock and decide if you can wait until the next break or not. In order to make that decision, you need a well-connected frontal lobe, or the front part of your brain. Most people don't think about it but the act of making a decision is represented in certain brain pathways in the front part of the brain. It's part of a term psychologists call executive functioning."

Noreen continued, "The brain is divided into four areas on each side of the brain. The front one is called, unsurprisingly, the frontal lobe." Noreen laughed at her own joke.

"Jake does not have an efficiently connected frontal lobe. On top of this, he has trouble saying words, or he might just get up and walk away. He can't stop the movement. Someone with ABA training might describe that as escape behavior or as being non-compliant of staying in his seat. One of the reasons I don't like the way ABA is practiced in autism is all of the behavior descriptions are negative terms, and they are often used in front of the kids. How would you feel if you walked around with people describing you as non-compliant, avoidant or attention- seeking? Especially if you could understand everything they were saying but were stuck in a body that didn't listen to your requests!?"

It explained a lot to Meg - a lot of the autism behavior she saw with Jake that is. Because he had a hard time learning or imitating new movements, he was stuck with the ones he had access to. Like playing with the See and Say toy. After several trials, Meg had taught him how to push the lever down, so he knew how to do it, but wasn't able to figure out how to play with other toys on his own.

Meg thought about the behavior clinic. It certainly did not appear to her that the staff presumed competence. They seemed to just repeat parts of a task they were trying to teach like buttoning pants or identifying numbers - ad nauseam. Jake had gotten better at buttoning his pants, but had been working on identifying the numbers 1-10 with little progress made over the past year. On top of that, she often observed the staff talking about the kids in front of them in a negative way as if it didn't matter because, of course they couldn't understand.

One particular episode came to mind as she thought about presuming competence. She remembered walking past a table where a child was sitting with a staff member who Meg especially enjoyed - she always seemed to have an upbeat attitude and talked to the kids respectfully. The young woman asked the student what color he wanted for a craft project they were working on. Another staff member walked by at that moment and quipped, rather harshly, "No point in asking him anything. He doesn't talk!" So disrespectful.

"Ahhh! Ahhhh!" She heard Jake in the back seat as they pulled into the clinic parking lot. Meg interpreted the vocalization as expressing displeasure at arriving at the clinic, and Meg considered just turning around and taking Jake home, but she couldn't afford to take the time off. Jake's dad had left a couple of years ago and he wasn't good at keeping up with child support, so she had to rely on herself. And, she was limited in her sick days.

Meg glanced back at Jake in the rear view mirror, then turned to look back at him directly. "Hey Jake. From everything we learned from Noreen yesterday, I'm thinking this is not the best place for you. I am going to call your support coordinator and some of our friends to start looking for a better place, but until then we'll have to keep coming here so I can go to work."

Meg reached out and touched Jake's leg as she saw him bring his hand to his mouth. In moments of deep frustration, Jake would bite his hands and forearms. Jake paused and looked into her eyes, seeming to understand exactly what she was saying.

He knew she was on his side, which gave Meg a sense of relief.

"I promise we will figure this out together, with a little help from our friends." Meg smiled, greeted by a similar smile back from Jake. Meg often tried to insert good song lyrics that Jake might know when she was talking to him. She had noticed it when she first inserted one of Joni Mitchell's lyrics in a conversation. She and a friend had been discussing autism research and how it was so confusing to know which way to go as all the professionals seemed to have differing advice. Meg had made a comment about "Being only particles of change", referring to the fact that, often, change can be really slow. Jake came out with a big belly laugh. One of his favorite albums to listen to was *Hejira* by Joni Mitchell. So began the tradition of inserting song lyrics into conversation.

Meg loved that, almost always, Jake seemed to get it and she in turn was able to enjoy his laugh, or at least a smile. Meg reaffirmed, "I promise we will figure this out. And, tonight I will read as many stories as you like!" Jake gave her a big grin in return for the offer.

Later that morning Jake was sitting at a table with his assigned assistant for the day, Teri. Jake liked Teri - she talked to him rather than about him, but he was getting pretty tired of all the M & Ms they used as his reward. Not to mention being bored at labeling the same pictures or numbers over and over.

Meg was starting to realize Jake knew what they were, he just had a hard time controlling which picture card he grabbed.

"Your mom told me you typed with someone yesterday!" Teri said. " I have heard about that, but have never seen it. Maybe you can show me one day!"

As Teri commented to Jake the director, Glen, walked by. "His mom said he typed?! That's a bunch of BS. Study after study has shown people with autism who don't talk also don't type. It's the person helping them, guiding them." Looking down at the pictures they were working on, he continued, "He isn't even correctly picking simple object pictures. How could he type a sentence?"

Teri stayed quiet, and Jake thought back to what Noreen had said yesterday, "It's not that you don't know things, it's that your body has a hard time moving how you want it to, especially when you are thinking about something."

He knew the picture cards as soon as he'd been shown them. His hand just seemed to have a mind of its own when he started reaching. It was like some zombie had taken control and he had nothing to say about it.

Jake really didn't like Dr. Donovan. He thought he could learn a thing or two, or ten for that matter, from Noreen.

Sharing A Good Joke

Later that afternoon Jake and his mom were back at Noreen's clinic. Noreen was a little surprised, though nothing should surprise her at this point, when Noreen pulled out Charlotte's Web to read to Jake.

Noreen had explained that the part of Jake's brain that processed certain visual information - objects, pictures but also whole words and their meaning, was well connected and working well, or maybe even overtime? Noreen had further explained, from what she had gathered over the years from typers, that it was as if his brain took a snapshot of what he was looking at and once that happened, he didn't forget. This is how Noreen thought Jake picked up on written words, particularly if those words were represented in meaningful ways. What they would work on now is to expand Jake's vocabulary while at the same time working on his motor control. Noreen began reading in a matter of fact but energetic way.

"Where's Papa going with that axe?" said Fern to her mother as they were setting the table for breakfast." Noreen read the first couple of paragraphs then set the book down face down on the table, briefly considering how her book loving friends would cringe, and picked up the white board.

Reading as she wrote, "What was Fern's dad going to do with the axe?"

Picking up another white board, Noreen wrote four choices, "Chop down a tree. Something else. Kill the runt. Practice his axe throwing." At this point Jake jumped up and shouted, seemingly in protest, his hand against his mouth, "AHHHHH!!"

"I know Jake. Sometimes emotional thoughts make it even harder to control your body, but that's also why it's important to practice talking about emotional things. It's like we have to practice controlling our bodies under different emotional circumstances. It's like how weightlifters lift progressively heavy weights. Each time they get stronger."

Noreen patted on the chair where Jake had been sitting. "When you're ready I want you to look at all the choices and only after you choose, select your choice. Thinking about it before you make your choice helps you control the movement. Right now thinking while making the choice is difficult for you, but with practice it will get easier and easier."

"It gets easier as we get older..." Meg chimed in with a smile, thinking of Willy Nelson's song "It get easier." And, Jake smiled and calmed a bit.

Noreen sat and waited while gesturing toward the empty chair seat beside her. After what felt to them all like a very long minute, Jake sat down and with Noreen squeezing just his forearm this time, chose "Kill the runt".

They went on like this, alternating reading and making choices, for another twenty minutes or so. Jake got every choice right, and Noreen was able to move up to just putting a hand on his shoulder as they got into a rhythm.

Next, Noreen pulled out the laminated letter board and held out her hand for Jake. "Is there anything you want to say Jake?"

After a moment, Jake put his hand into Noreen's and pointed to the letters, I THINK I WANT TO BE FRIENDS WITH FERN AND WILBUR.

"Me too!" agreed Noreen.

"Me three!" Meg thirded the sentiment.

A big smile crossed Jake's face and he rocked back and forth in his chair a bit. It felt so good to be able to share his thoughts - to actually have a conversation!

They went back and forth talking about Wilbur and Fern's friendship and then Jake got an idea. He reached for Noreen's hand and she held it out for him. With a smile splitting his face, Jake typed, " What did the pig decide to do on a summer day?"

"No idea. What did he do?" Noreen smiled and held out her hand.

"They went to a pig-nic!" Jake giggled as he typed and Noreen laughed.

As they finished off their session for the afternoon, Noreen went over the layout of how their sessions would progress. In their next session, she wanted to bring Meg into the mix more, to have her feel and practice how to give Jake support. Meg was nervous, but excited. She had already been using the white board with choices some with Jake and that was going pretty well, but he had balked every time she brought out the letter board.

Expert Opinion

Abuse Allegations, Influence And Motor Theories.

Most probably the initial impetus behind the controversy with supported typing, in 1992 the first of several abuse allegations came out using facilitated communication, prompting the scientific community to study who was doing the typing.

> In February of 1993 *An Experimental Assessment of Facilitated Communication* was published in the *Mental Retardation* Journal. This study, done at the O.D. Heck Developmental Center in New York used blind conditions, where the typer and facilitator were shown different pictures sometimes, with a long board between them so they couldn't see what the other was being shown.

Under these conditions, it was clear that there was obvious influence by the facilitator. In other words, when shown two different pictures, what was typed was what the facilitator saw. Several similarly set up studies showed similar results. Many said that was all that was happening here, that what was being typed was simply what the therapist guided the person to type, and this continues to this day. For example, in his 2005 paper criticizing Facilitated Communication, Lilienfield describes FCT as "a facilitator who *guides* their [the typer's] hand movements", which is not true, if done correctly.

An Experimental Assessment of Facilitated Communication, Wheeler, Douglas L; Jacobson, John W; Paglieri, Raymond A; Schwartz, Allen A. Mental Retardation; Washington, etc. Vol. 31, Iss. 1,(Feb 1, 1993): 49.

Interestingly, decades later a 2023 study showed, using linguistic analysis, that communications were reflective of *both* facilitator and typer, suggesting there is influence, but also true communication from the person with autism. Further, despite numerous autobiographical books by individuals who became independent with typing using these strategies; numerous qualitative studies and books; and numerous experimental studies evidencing motor difficulties in persons with autism, professional organizations, the American Speech Language and Hearing Association for one example, to caution people against using this technique. It is highly probable that any family wanting to use supported typing gets a lot of pushback if they ask for support in the schools. In this piece I review important points in this controversy.

Nicoli, G., Pavon, G., Grayson, A., Emerson, A., Cortelazzo, M., & Mitra, S. (2023).Individuals with developmental disabilities make their own stylistic contributions to text written with physical facilitation. Frontiers in Child and Adolescent Psychiatry, 2, 1182884.

Prisoners Of Silence

In October of 1993 *Frontline* airs a documentary, *Prisoners of Silence* where they detail the controversy. In *Prisoners of Silence* you get a feel for the frenzy that must have happened when Facilitated Communication was introduced in the United States. Conferences and trainings attracted hundreds of attendees. Of course it would. If true, this would be, or has been, life changing for individuals.

But the abuse allegations combined with studies that evidenced influence with what is typed, and little understanding as to why, led some to determine that all that was happening was a Ouija board phenomenon. On the other side, therapists and mothers who had first hand experiences didn't give up and believed there was much more to understand. But, as I have stated, the debate over the years has been harsh.

To illustrate, a 2023 paper by Dan Howitt picks apart a video from a 60 *Minutes* segment showing Soma supporting Tito to type. Rather than objectively trying to understand the totality of this strategy, the video is picked apart for ways that Soma could be cueing Tito. Howitt even argues in his paper :

Soma desires to publicly portray Tito as a miracle, and to publicly portray herself as a miracle worker; and in order to accomplish this, she engages in, and continues to engage in, the novel, highly surreptitious, multifaceted, communicative deception that I revealed, and which has evaded the millions of viewers of them over the last approximate twenty-three years, including the vast array of scientists, physicians, other clinicians, journalists, autism organization leaders, etc., who studied them (Merzenich et al., 2008). In so doing, Soma, with regard to Tito, engages in Factitious Heroism By Proxy, as she, via her deception, portrays him as accomplishing something (that is, as being a "miracle") in order that he is admired by other people, and in order that she encounters immense gratification. Moreover, Soma engages in Factitious Heroism, as she portrays herself as being the hero (that is, the "miracle worker") of the accomplishment that she presents Tito as having accomplished.

It is no wonder the folks who developed these techniques might be wary of the public eye. It is important to note here that the article Howitt cites is by a world renowned neuroscience researcher, Michael Merzenich, who spent hours with Tito, doing research over a year. On a 60 minutes segment about Tito and supported typing Merzenich says, "I think there could be thousands, maybe tens of thousands of Titos out there." On the other hand, that I know of, Howitt never met Tito.

In a later vignette we will go into further detail about the cueing/influence and why it makes sense from a neurologic perspective. It is important to note that I do observe some of the cueing Howitt observes with Soma and Tito, but whereas Howitt suggests all that is happening is Soma cueing what Tito types, I assume that Soma was trying to support Tito.

For example, at one point it looks like Soma wrote a sentence starter for Tito to complete. Howitt claims that Soma practiced this to the point where Tito was cued with the sentence starter to complete the sentence as Soma "dictated" and practiced with him. But in my mind, I have found over the years that when questions are asked, some typers have a hard time remembering the question as they are typing - a memory issue, not an understanding one. Whereas Howitt assumes Soma is engaging in what he calls "factitious heroism," I believe this was one of Tito's earlier interviews, and he likely needed more support.

Although Tito types, he still experiences autism with its accompanying challenges, including dysregulation.

I invite the reader to watch one more video of Tito, comparing it to the Howitt video five years earlier. Five years later, after much more practice and experience, Tito is clearly able to  answer questions, asked spontaneously, and there are no "cues so subtle only a trained eye can see them", or at least not this trained eye.

Howitt, Dan (2023) The Case of Tito and Soma Mukhopadhyay: Factitious Heroism by Proxy, Factitious Heroism, and Revealing the Deception Thereof for the Future of Autism Treatment. Future Human Image, Volume 20, 55-72. https://doi.org/10.29202/fhi/20/6

Influence, External Cues And Supported Typing

The first facilitators were not aware of all of the pitfalls, mostly the potential for influence. In order to better understand how autistic people might be unusually susceptible to influence, let's consider first how autistic kids learn and navigate their environment. Kids with autism are unusually reliant on external cueing such as verbal direction or physical prompts to learn new movements (**see Prompt**

dependency in ABA), but, I think, this *also* makes them especially susceptible to influence. Because professionals doing the initial trainings were unaware of the strength of this pitfall, they were less aware of how much a slight lean in one direction could affect typer accuracy. After they became aware of the cueing, the focus was more on the road to independent typing, but critics suggested even here that the typers were picking up on subtle cues from someone standing in the room. Of the independent typers presented in this book, I will leave it to the reader to decide if the person is actually typing their thoughts or they are solely picking up on subtle cues to know which letter to type.

Further, I believe, many of the autistic folks who participated in the trainings were able to pick up on the written word, but didn't have the capacity yet to pass a test done with blinding conditions done with visual or auditory blocks - whether it be word finding, memory difficulties or body challenges/susceptibility to influence. But one important aspect of supported typing that contradicts the narrative that supported typing is simply guiding the typer's movement is the calm engagement observed by typers - despite regulation challenges participants in the studies, *nevertheless* sat and participated.

Donnellan and Leary describe it well:

> ….aspects of what we were observing astonished us…. People who had never in their lives remained focused on a single interactional activity for more than a few minutes were willingly and attentively doing something intensely social for long stretches of

time. Generally, they did not seem to need external rewards, behavioral contingencies or even much coaching to stay with the activity.

Donnellan, A. M., & Leary, M. R. (1995). Movement Differences and Diversity in Autism-Mental Retardation: Appreciations and Accommodations People With Communications and Behavior Challenges. *DRI press*.

When I first was 'trained' in facilitated communication it was by a speech therapist. She spent *maybe* ten minutes showing me how to resist the person's arm at the hand. There was no training on body mechanics (I have found even leaning slightly in one direction can influence what is being typed); how to hold the board or other pitfalls to be wary of - no warning about influence. And, while there is no doubt in my mind that Kris typed "Raffi" with me, I also have no doubt that he would not have sat still for a twenty object naming task. I have questioned that the participants were "naturally" selected in that these were individuals who could sit for the time of the study. Many people I know with autism would not be able to stay regulated, at least in the beginning part of their typing journey.

Another factor to consider regarding the influence, there is a syndrome called **institutional syndrome** or institutionalization where after a long time being in an institution there is a loss of individuality with an increase in passiveness, apathy, submissiveness and compliance. Because the testing required participants to sit and finish the test, it is possible there was some biased selection on participants who were more submissive and compliant, and thus more susceptible to influence.

When I was in graduate school I took an independent study course, which entailed reading a book, *The neural basis of motor control*, and writing a paper. Though I had entered school determined to keep a low profile, knowing the controversy, and not bring up facilitated communication, I also knew my main goal was to learn as much as I could about the motor system and the autism brain in hopes of finding a strong rationale for why we saw what we do in supported typing. I trusted the professor I was working with enough to choose the controversy as my subject. The paper I ended up writing for this independent study was where I began my theory on the neurology of supported typing. The paper was titled, *Crossley and Wheeler. Maybe they're both right?* In other words, Rosemary Crossley was right in that giving resistance supported people to type, but that same support could influence what was being typed.

Detractors have compared supported typing to the story of Clever Hans. Clever Hans was a horse whose owner had taught him math. He would stomp his hoof the number of times when given a number. But when they looked at this closer, the horse seemed to be stopping only when the owner would shift his weight forward, suggesting the horse didn't know math but was relying on cues from his owner.

Now, at first glance this might seem to explain the influence.

Yet, many of the folks who support the idea that supported typing is *only* the facilitator guiding, also say that facilitators who are standing next to or even in the same room as a typer, who is typing without anyone touching, are giving subtle cues for the person to type. This *might* be reasonable if we were talking about people with typical nervous systems - typical people are able to regulate and sit for twenty minutes without someone touching them. Beyond just being able to sit for an extended period, I am sure it would take me a lot of practice to learn which of 26 letters to type based on a slight shrug of a shoulder or head tilt- and I am not even sure I could do it.

Detractors suggest that these individuals, many of whom they say are severely intellectually impaired, can learn which letters to type based on a subtle change in posture by their support person. If they are right, I would suggest this is a skill that *someone* should do a study on.

However, I believe a more likely explanation would be that the people with autism who type 1) Have picked up on some written language, but haven't mastered *all* language and beyond this there are memory and processing differences; 2) These folks have dyspraxia and visuomotor challenges that make it hard for them to access a keyboard independently and so they need prompts to support their motor system; and 3) The very prompts or supports they need to access the keyboard are also the same supports that can influence what is being typed, compounded by a nervous system that is especially susceptible to influence or **thigmotaxis**.

So, What Is Praxis?

Praxis, confusingly, may be defined differently, depending on your occupation. Generally, we can think of praxis as the ability to perform skilled or learned movements, and, from a developmental standpoint, also the ability learn these skills.

Apraxia, then, is a disorder of intentional movement that cannot be accounted for by primary motor and sensory deficits, comprehension, attentional, or motivational deficits. Apraxia is the term behavioral neurologists use with persons who have had a stroke, while developmental dyspraxia is when it happens as a result of atypical brain development in a child. Though, it should be noted, that the term apraxia is often used in developmental disorders, especially autism - making it even more confusing at times.

Because most recent studies in autism have looked at difficulties with praxis using the tests they use for adults, and the underlying neuroanatomy of autistic persons aligns with the areas of the brain damaged in someone who has had a stroke and has apraxia, I consider this body of research and definition when talking about dyspraxia in autism.

To explain further, physical and occupational therapists often use the **Sensory Integration and Praxis Test (SIPT)** to evaluate for difficulty with praxis using meaningless movements such as slapping your knee five times then clapping your hands. This would measure your ability to imitate movements, your ability to learn *new* movements. While imitation is one component of praxis, the recent autism studies have looked at ability to gesture things like brushing your teeth or give me a thumbs up - movements with meaning, movements which use different brain connections than imitation. Behavioral neurologists who study praxis call difficulties with praxis in children *developmental dyspraxia*, because it's not so much that a person has lost the ability, more that they don't have strong neural connections to develop this in the first place. Maybe most importantly, these studies have also looked at *understanding* of the task. For example, if you can't pantomime drinking out of a cup, but you can make the movement if the actual cup is there, this demonstrates understanding. Now that we have a better understanding of praxis, let's look at how motor differences in autism were first addressed.

Early Motor Theories

One of the first books to address the movement differences seen in autism and mental retardation, *Movement Differences and Diversity in Autism/Mental Retardation: Appreciations and Accommodations People With Communications and Behavior Challenges,* was published in 1994. Authors include Anne Donnellan, a special education professor and Martha Leary, a speech therapist. Leary and Donnellan review the history of intelligence testing and propose rather than having a theory of intelligence that implies a person isn't capable of learning or has diminished capacity to learn, it may serve those we serve better if we think of our clients as different learners with impediments to learning.

Donnellan and Leary then review the study and progression of movement differences in person's with psychiatric diagnoses, including those seen in autism.

Part of their discussion is centered around the book and subsequent movie, *Awakenings*. For those of you who need a refresher, the story in *Awakenings* centers around Oliver Sacks' experience with people institutionalized after having had encephalitis. In the early 1900s there was an encephalitis epidemic and many people had unusual symptoms, such as catatonia, and were institutionalized. When Sacks gave them L-Dopa, a drug used in Parkinson's, the patients were able to awake and symptoms dissipated - though only for a period of time before the L-Dopa either stopped working or there were bad side effects.

Donnellan and Leary lay out the movement symptoms of catatonia, many of which are seen in persons with autism and mental retardation, and then refer to 1991 research by Rogers and colleagues. Rogers' study looked at whether these movement differences were fully attributable to side effects of medications as many physicians had thought. Instead, they found that even people not taking the medications had these movement differences, suggesting that there was an underlying neurological reason for the movement differences.

Rogers, D., Karki, C., Bartlett, C., & Pocock, P. (1991). The motor disorders of mental handicap: An overlap with the motor disorders of severe psychiatric illness. *The British Journal of Psychiatry, 158*(1), 97-102.

Leary and Donnellan go on to discuss the "problem behaviors" seen in autism - are these behaviors intentional? They use an example of a young man, Bob, with autism who recently had an increase in behaviors of flapping his hands, swearing or saying challenging things to others. He often would laugh after doing these behaviors, making staff attribute intentionality. Donnellan and Leary point out that many of these behaviors were possible movement disturbance symptoms - for example Bob may have had a hard time inhibiting swearing or flapping his hands. It may be a little challenging to understand how swearing or flapping your hands can be looked at as a movement disorder, so let's look at that a little closer.

Swearing. Verbal speech comes from neural circuits or loops in the front part of the brain, discussed more below. These pathways support you to stop, start and inhibit speech and movements but also thoughts and emotions. So we can think of inappropriate swearing as difficulty inhibiting speech in these pathways. As regards hand flapping, imaging studies show strong representation of U loops that connect adjacent areas of the brain. Explained further below, there is autobiographical and imaging evidence that if an autistic person flaps their arms it increases their body awareness. Importantly, Donnellan and Leary point out that when you approach autism as a symptom of movement disturbance, you take away the blame and then have an opportunity to work with the person to figure out accommodations, with respect, in order to decrease the behavior.

The spirit of intervention and the faith that he will be able to regain self control are in contrast to the traditional view that the program changed his behavior or he found out he could "not get away with that" anymore.

Donnellan and Leary (1994) acknowledge that our knowledge is limited about how developmental movement differences affect learning, but suggest the least dangerous assumption is to assume these differences *do* affect learning.

Donnellan and Leary talk about the circular thinking when it comes to autism. Someone flaps their hands and has difficulties with speaking so we say they are autistic. A parent asks why their child doesn't talk. It's because he has autism is the answer. Donnellan and Leary go on to suggest asking questions like "Why is this person able to talk sometimes and sometimes they are not able?" will give better answers than "because he is retarded or because he has autism."

They propose difficulties with initiating, inhibiting and sustaining movement, but also difficulties with initiating, inhibiting and sustaining speech, thoughts and emotions. The neural circuits in the frontal lobe called **frontostriatal (FSC)** connections are an area of study in obsessive compulsive disorders and the repetitive movements seen in autism. These are the pathways that represent any over learned habit.

Dysfunction in the FSC can lead to personality changes, including: emotional lability, behavioral disinhibition, aggressive outbursts, poor judgment, and lack of interpersonal sensitivity as well as difficulties with movement.

Donnellan and Leary lay out insightful examples of ways to reconsider looking at autism - different ways to interpret what we see. They talk about automatic movements vs volitional movement and the difficulty persons with autism have in using volitional movements. For example, I have met many people with autism who jump as a form of "self stim" (automatic) yet if you ask the person to jump on command (volitional), they can't.

Drawing partly from ABA therapies, Donnellan Leary suggest accommodations for the movement difficulties seen in autism such as rhythm, touch, music or verbal cues. These accommodations were the initial basis for our therapeutic approach at Kris' Camp, an intensive therapy and respite program that approaches autism as a sensory motor difference. For example, we might start our day in a music group where campers practice starting stopping and sustaining movements with supports. Maybe most important, many parents tell us that one of the things they find the most unusual at Kris' Camp is the way we talk to the kids - like they understand everything we say. As Donnellan and Leary suggest, the *least dangerous assumption* is to assume competence and support the motor differences.

Follow The Money

Later that evening Jake and his mom were back at the ABA clinic for their third night of the week. Jake never really liked being at the clinic, especially since his work with Noreen brought a stark contrast to his work at the clinic. While Noreen seemed to understand his unique intelligence, Jake felt most of the staff at the behavior clinic thought he was stupid, retarded - how he hated that word. Jake was metaphorically holding his breath waiting for his mom to find a new place for him.

While his mom cleaned, Jake watched some videos on a tablet. After working with Noreen, Meg had turned on the captions which Jake loved. He could now enjoy his videos while at the same time picking up on a few new words! Jake found it very relaxing to see the words. It felt like he was drinking water after a long walk on a hot day. Jake wondered if it had anything to do with his word brain pathway being well connected as compared to his thinking motor pathway. Like going down a wet slippery slide vs going down a slide hot from the sunshine with a sweaty bottom.

As Meg moved around cleaning the clinic, she brought Jake with her. There was a bean bag chair he liked to sit in so Meg just moved it around with her as she moved so she could keep an eye on Jake. As such, Jake found himself seated in the bean bag in a corner of Glen Donovan's office. As the video ended, Jake got up, standing in front of Glen's desk. There were ledgers strewn about and Jake picked one up and flipped through the pages, holding the ledger close to his face. Doing this, Jake's brain took what he thought of as snapshots - once he saw something he didn't forget, like his brain took a snapshot. In this particular ledger there seemed to be a series of invoices, and Jake noticed one for one of his fellow students, Otto, for the past month. But, Otto had left months ago? Why was there a bill for this month?

I Just Want Them Dead!

Glen hung up the phone and muttered to himself, again. "Damn imbecile..." He was mystified at the incompetence of the hit man that was sent to kill Daisy. He would have to go a different route and hire the other, substantially more expensive, guys.

I guess you get what you pay for! Glen thought to himself as he leafed through the ledgers on his desk. He had been working on figuring out how to come up with the extra monies he needed, and he had an idea. He had some individuals who had left the center but still had some money on their plan. If he continued to bill for them, how much could he make up?

Glen walked out back of the center to make the call. There was a fenced in playground beyond the back parking lot and he noticed two of the kids in the playground, Jake and Nick. He knew that oftentimes when the assistants went on a break they brought these two back to the playground and watched them from the window inside the break room. Both were fairly well regulated, were calmer in the outdoors and the staff seemed to think they were friends. Of course Glen had his own ideas on that, but he didn't see the harm.

He walked around to the other side of the fence to make his phone call. He wasn't worried about the kids hearing him.

There was nothing they could do about it even if they did understand him.

Standing in front of the tic tac toe game that was a part of the playground equipment, Jake gently spun the Xs and Os -

he liked the spinnability of the games, Jake could hear the anger and frustration in Glen's voice and froze at his words. "I just want them dead, and the sooner the better!"

For Glen, of course, his disdain for the supported typing craze had started with the abuse allegation his nephew had made against his brother. Then, he met Noreen at an autism continuing education conference. Noreen was a very attractive woman and Glen quickly developed a huge crush.

Glen had courted Noreen for a bit after that conference and had even caved a little on his views on supported typing. But in the end Noreen was not interested and their brief encounter ended. Glen had never let go of his anger at being rejected, compounded by the fact that he and Noreen found themselves squaring off on opposite sides of the supported typing debate. It wasn't long after that conference that he started writing opinion pieces and recommendations, in terms of whether supported typing should be used (or not), to any media outlet or professional organization who would listen.

He had spearheaded efforts with ASHA, the International Society for Augmentative and Alternative Communication (ISAAC) and the American Pediatric Association. He was successful with all three in getting them to put out a statement that the supported typing techniques were discredited techniques and possibly dangerous.

To Glen there was no hidden intelligence for what he referred to, more than once, as those imbeciles. What had started off as a mild irritant eventually turned into a full blown obsession for Glen after the accusations of abuse;

studies that showed the facilitator was guiding what was typed; and his failed attempt to date Noreen. A small part of him knew he should be over it by now, but he wasn't.. He had vowed to himself that he wouldn't give up until he shut them down, or died trying.

It wasn't just views of supported typing that he was on opposite sides with the typing people. He also knew that the supported typing community was solidly against using any kind of electric shock treatments. Daisy had even been on the opposing side when he had testified in front of congress a few years back.

Donovan had been approached by a behavior analyst colleague about developing an electric shock appliance for kids who banged their heads or bit their hands and he had gladly accepted being part of the team. He didn't get why people got so up in arms about it. Granted, their had been some incidents of death and hospitalizations that had happened due to the restraint and shocks, but he had made up his mind several years into his career that he had had enough of getting hit, bit and pinched, and he felt it was a totally reasonable approach to dealing with the "head bangers" as he called them. He had convinced himself electric shock was a reasonable tool to help stop that. He had totally lost it. It didn't matter to Glen if some students got hurt.

Jake's Opportunity

Today was the day that they were going to focus on supporting Meg to support Jake to type. Meg had been using the white boards as Noreen had shown her, but they were waiting to try the typing until Meg had the chance to practice with Noreen's guidance. Well, Noreen had suggested she wait, but Meg couldn't resist bringing the letter board to Jake. Thing was, he didn't seem to want to type with her. Instead, he pushed the board away and cried. So, Meg decided to wait until after she'd had more practice with Noreen.

Noreen situated Meg and Jake in chairs side by side with Meg turned slightly towards Jake. Noreen explained how it was important for the facilitator to be in a good position in terms of body mechanics. They had learned over the years that even a slight leaning in one direction or another, or where you placed the letter board could add to the possibility of influence.

Meg was nervous. Though she had used the white board with Jake, and that had gone well, supporting Jake to type letters seemed far more complicated and Meg was terrified she might influence what he typed.

Meg voiced her concern to Jake and Noreen. "I'm a little worried you guys. Noreen, I know we said to wait but I did offer the letter board to Jake a couple of times just to try and he pushed it away. I'm afraid you don't want to type with me, Jake. Or, that maybe I might not be giving you the right support. "

"That's totally normal. Or, at least very common." said Noreen. "I have a good friend, Sheila, who has typed with her son since he was five and he's now twenty-five." Noreen paused and smiled, "But, when they first started typing, Sheila had to chase Jerry around with the letter board, insisting he type. Each family has been different in terms of challenges they face, but on the whole, it is more difficult to get into a pattern. I think it is partly the relationship - you guys have developed your own way of communicating and it's a little..." Noreen paused, debating on her next word, "... freaky to all of a sudden communicate with typing. Plus, " Noreen added, "The majority of my parents have little experience as therapists. I used to think my therapy could easily be taught in one session. But I have learned over the years it truly is a skill that takes time to learn. You wouldn't expect to be proficient on playing the piano after one lesson, or to drive a car, so why should this be any different?"

Noreen sat in a chair opposite Jake and Meg. "I have found that if you keep up with it, there will be a gradual ease with it. At first it might be one word that Jake is clear on spelling, and really wants to tell you. But, you will eventually settle into a routine. I have total confidence."

Hearing Noreen's reassuring words in her calm matter-of-fact voice calmed Meg's nerves.

"So, let's start with something that's pretty dry and simple. We're going to do some copy typing so you can get the feel of it with less pressure. Then we'll progress to fill in the blanks." Noreen put a stack of index cards and took four cards off the top of the pile and turned them over. CHEESE. REFRIGERATOR. MOUNTAIN. PEACE.

"Ok Jake, first we'll have you pick a word you want to type.

Then, Meg, you'll support Jake to type the word. We'll start using physical support, resistance to the arm, which is how I first learned to support."

Noreen continued, "I used that method for years, but then other methods came out and I've incorporated some of the elements of those methods to mix it up so that folks don't get stuck on a certain method. Sometimes kids get stuck on needing the physical support, and the other methods rely more on object and verbal cues. The general thought is it's good to do things differently so you don't get over reliant on any certain way. In this way it will help Jake to get to a place of independence - or at least in theory!"

Noreen brought out the laminated letter board and handed it to Meg. She pushed her chair over so she was sitting next to Meg and turned slightly towards her. "What I want you to do is to push back against my hand. I learned from another therapist who was studying the neurology of autism in graduate school that there are short brain connections that are called U-loops.

They connect each adjacent area of the brain, and are activated any time you use your muscles - move your body or push against resistance.

"I love a quote from a guy I know who types to communicate. He said 'I don't feel my hand unless I feel your hand on my hand. I don't feel my feet unless I'm stomping them.' My friend has this long-winded neurologic explanation, but I love the quote because it shows how movement and the sense of touch can help with body awareness and then motor accuracy. Can you imagine what it must feel like if you don't have a sense of where your body is unless your moving it? I think that's why we see such active intention when we give the resistance. They aren't sensing as clearly where their arm and hand is until you activate their muscles with the resistance."

Noreen leaned forward and took ahold of Meg's hand. "I am going to push back against you as you type. I want you to type the word SUCCESS."

Meg pushed forward and was surprised at how much resistance she felt. In researching more about supported typing Meg had come across several web pages, mostly negative. Most of the references suggested that the person supporting was guiding the typer's hand, but this wasn't that at all!" Meg typed the word SUCCESS. As she moved forward she felt Noreen ease up a bit in her resistance.

"I've heard the analogy that it's like driving a stick shift. You start off pushing harder then slowly let up." Noreen explained.

Noreen pushed her chair back and gestured for Meg to turn towards Jake and offered him some word choices on a white board. "Jake, I want you to choose a word." After about ten seconds, Noreen touched Jake on the shoulder and said, "Think about choosing a word." Jake reached out and chose the word INCREDIBLE.

"So Meg I want you to put your hand out and offer it to Jake like you saw me do. Then resist and type the word!"

As Meg turned and offered her hand to Jake he started biting his arm, well more that he mouthed his arm - he didn't really bite unless he was really upset. Then he reached out for Meg's hair.

"No!" Meg cried out, calmly but forcefully and Jake pulled his hands back.

Meg took a deep breath and ginned up the confidence she heard in her voice, "Ok. Jake. We got this! We'll work through this together!"

Jake calmed for a moment and Noreen tried to reassure them, "It's ok. Just remember - this is different and it will take some getting used to."

At that Jake promptly, and at the speed of lightning, grabbed Meg's hair and pulled her face so their noses were touching.

Meg was used to this and calmly pushed in on Jakes hands as she spoke, and he let go. " It's ok. We got this Jake."

Without skipping a beat, Noreen leaned in as Jake settled himself back in his chair.. "Ok. Let's try that again." Noreen's voice was calm and soothing. It was no wonder many of her clients were so drawn to Noreen. One even called her the beacon, as in beacon of hope.

Noreen had placed the INCREDIBLE word card on the table in front of Meg and Jake. "Remember, try and situate the board so that Jake's hand is equidistant to each letter. We will first try it with resistance, then we'll move on to a different method."

Meg offered her hand again to Jake and this time he reached for it. Jake, with Meg's resistance support, typed out INCREDIBLE. Meg's eyes widened. It was one thing to watch Noreen with Jake, but it was an entirely different thing to feel the clear intentionality as Jake pushed against her hand.

They then went through the method of handing Jake a pencil and he used the pencil to push through letters in a stencil board. Jake had picked the word PIGNIC as a wry smile crossed his face at Noreen's reference to his joke the first day they typed.

"Next I'm going to read you something and then we'll have you fill in the blanks, Jake." Noreen picked a paper she had written notes on and smiled. Her eyes held a twinkle as she looked at Meg and Jake. "What did the blanket say when she fell off the bed?"

Noreen paused waiting for the answer - tickled at the puzzled look on Meg's face. "I have no idea!"

"Oh sheet!" Noreen answered and they all giggled. "One of my life mottos is you can never laugh enough!"

Noreen pointed to the stencil board. "Ok. So who asked the question in this joke?"

Meg took the pencil and handed it to Jake who grabbed it automatically. Jake pointed the pencil toward the board and went to the O but then dropped the pencil. Meg reached down for the pencil and handed it back to Jake. "Almost! I saw you getting close to it try again!"

This time Jake went a little to the right of where the N was and Meg coached him. "A little to the left." and he was able to push through the empty N space in the stencil board then the O.

"You've got it!" Noreen cheered them on. "When you're supporting Jake, they recommend you don't touch him, but instead coach him with your words where to go. The idea with this method is that Jake is working on his controlled intentional movement. The idea is that when the movement becomes automatic, it dissociates the movement from the thinking. For whatever reason neurologically, adding the thinking, or even just heightened emotions, makes it that much harder to control. You know how your knees shake when you are nervous, like when you're speaking in front of a large group? You can't will it to stop." Noreen continued, "It's like that - you have little, if any, control.

"The movement piece is what seems to be so difficult for people to wrap their heads around. But when you start to consider things we see in autism, it starts to make sense. For example, many people with autism jump. For some, it's pretty constant. A guy in Japan even wrote a book about it, *The reason I Jump*! But, if you ask that same person to jump on command, they can't do it. Jumping automatically vs jumping on command are two different tasks. We don't think about it that way, but they are!

"Another way to think about the automatic vs on command, or thinking movement, is when the date changes at the beginning of a new year. I don't know about you, but it takes me a good month before writing the new year becomes automatic.

Before that, you find yourself having to autocorrect as you start writing 2023 instead of 2024."

Noreen paused and stared off for a moment, thinking. "I've heard people who question the typing stuff suggest that because someone with autism can type in their pin code at warp speed, they can't have a movement disorder. I think the reason the typer can type their pin code is at this point it's an automatic.

What's different is that it may take longer, and with LOTS more practice, to learn a new code. So, for you or I it may take a month of us self-correcting to get automatic with the new year, while it may take someone with autism two months or more with lots of support to type the new code."

Noreen worked with Meg and Jake for several more minutes, alternating between stencil board and letter board, reading and typing. Then Noreen asked Jake if he had anything more to say and offered him the choices of I DO and I DO NOT. Jake chose I DO, leaning forward in his chair and then immediately jumped up and ran across the room, his hand flapping against his mouth, letting out a distressed cry, "BWAHH! BWAHH!!"

It was significant to Meg that the tone of Jake's voice seemed different since they had been working with Noreen. Before Jake had worked with Noreen his cries were more vague, or at least that's how Meg would describe it. But now, you could hear tones of anger, frustration, sadness when Jake made his vocalizations. It was as if he realized just how smart he was, and now knew he had an avenue to communicate and it was their job - Meg and Noreen's, to figure it out.

Meg couldn't help but take it a little personally. She wondered if Jake jumped up because he didn't want to type with her. But Noreen took over. "Ok Jake, I hear you sounding a little anxious about something."

Noreen walked over to Jake and gave both his hands deep rhythmic squeezes, something she had found helped with regulation, as she spoke to Jake, "I want you to get your eyes on the chair and think about sitting down."

Jake had quieted and walked over and sat down. Meg had stood up as Noreen offered the regulation support to Jake and Noreen slid into the chair next to Jake.

"I have found over the years that once you get out whatever it is that is causing you upset, for whatever reason, it helps you calm . Kind of like when you have a good cry. That same therapist I was talking to you about who knows her neurology told me that tears of emotion have a natural pain reliever. If I remember correctly I think oxytocin is one of them. Anyway, that's why the old saying about feeling better after "having a good cry" makes sense."

Noreen got out the letter board and offered her hand to Jake. "What do you want to say?'

Jake, calm but with a determined look in his eyes, reached for Noreen's hand and typed, "HE IS STEALING!"

Noreen furrowed her brow, "Who is stealing, Jake?"

Jake typed, "Glen. Medicald." Jake misspelled medicaid, but Noreen and Meg easily got what he meant.

"Is there more?" asked Noreen.

Jake typed, "KILL" then promptly jumped up and began his regulation routine again. "BWAHH! BWAHH!"

Meg and Noreen sat, stunned by what Jake had typed. What in the world can he possibly mean? Kill what? Kill who?

Noreen, Meg and Jake spent the next twenty minutes, going over the session time by fifteen minutes, trying to figure out what Jake was trying to tell them. This was one of the most frustrating times for Noreen. When a new typer had something important they wanted to share, but they couldn't get it out.

Maybe it was they didn't quite have the right words, or maybe the emotional importance compounded their movement difficulties? Probably a combination of both.

Either way, after alternating regulation strategies with attempts at communication, all that they were able to understand was Jake seemed to think someone wanted to kill. But each time they tried to understand more, Jake got very emotional and they had to stop typing.

After their last attempt, Noreen silently walked over to Jake, took hold of his hands and gave him the calming rhythmic squeezes. "It sounds like you have something you want us to understand, and we will, but for right right now it's time to close our session. I have a standing appointment near Big Bear, so I won't be available tomorrow, but let's work something in for Thursday so we can talk more."

Jake calmed down enough for Meg to shepherd him to the car. As she left the clinic Noreen and she exchanged a puzzled glance. And, as Jake sat in his seat, Meg closed the car door and whispered to Noreen, "I have no idea what he's trying to say, but please be careful. I would hate for something to happen to you!" Then Meg impulsively gave Noreen a big bear hug.

Noreen laughed, "I'm pretty tough! But, yes, I'll be careful.

You be careful too!"

Noreen's Mountain Drive

Noreen reflected back on Jake's words as she drove the two hours plus across multiple highways and then up the mountain to Big Bear, California. She had a couple of parents who combined resources and started a group home for persons with autism, including their sons. They had bought an old log cabin and made it into an inviting home for their kids.

Outside, at Adam's request, hung several wind chimes of various sizes. Inside, much to Noreen's delight, were comfy oversized chairs and several large bean bags. Most of the clients had the diagnosis of autism except for one guy, Charlie, whose mom was good friend's with Adam's mom, Kate. He had athetoid cerebral palsy and communicated by using a switch he used with his knees. From what Noreen observed, the other clients had great affection for Charlie. It was easy to see why.

Charlie was one of those people that Noreen thought of as an old soul. Even though Charlie couldn't speak words out of his mouth, his eyes, frequently holding a glimmer, told you all you needed to know about his brightness and sense of humor.

"Knock knock!" Noreen called out as she entered the house. "We're out back!" Noreen heard Gail, one of the regular staff, call out to her.

Behind the facility there was a huge screened in porch with several rocking chairs and bean bags. Several hanging baskets filled with Bougainvillea and Arizona Yellow Bell flowers. There was a beautiful view of mountains and Joni Mitchell's Ladies of the Canyon played on a blue tooth speaker. Adam's favorite album. And, the smell of mountain pines in the summer completed the scene.

"How is everyone today?" asked Noreen as she walked out on the patio and took a deep breath. "Ahh! So much better than the smog over LA!"'

Noreen walked over to a big table and started pulling things from her travel bag. She had a poetry book they were going to read from today, and then discuss it. They alternated who picked the reading, with Noreen filling in if no one had made a choice. Noreen had picked a poem about disability that she thought would be ripe for discussion. It was hopeful if a little sad, but she thought it would spark some good conversation.

Adam walked over as Noreen laid copies of the poem in front of chairs around the table and reached out and gently touched the top of Noreen's head. Adam had such a gentle manner about him, and even though he couldn't speak, he was obviously saying hello to Noreen and giving her a gentle hug. Or, at least that was Noreen's interpretation.

As Noreen laid out the items, Gail gathered up the clients and guided them to sit at the table. Noreen picked up the poem, "You guys might find this a bit sad, but it was written by one of my clients with autism who typed and he wanted me to share it with you, to get your opinion."

"Before we start", Noreen continued, "Who wants to do some deep pressure squeezes?" She had several pairs of laminated cards that had the words YES and NO written on them and she and Gail went around the group and registered each vote.

The group voted yes for squeezes and Noreen and Gail went around and gave deep rhythmic squeezes first to the client's feet, then up the legs to the head, shoulders and finally down the arms to the hands. Noreen had some music therapist colleagues who had made up some "squeeze songs", which Noreen sang as they rotated between clients, adding in verses so all the clients could receive the deep pressure. Of all sensory strategies Noreen had tried over the years, Noreen found her clients, pretty much across the board, loved the deep pressure squeezes. So, Noreen had incorporated the squeezes as a prep to typing conversations.

"So, I picked this poem out as I thought it would spark some good conversation." explained Noreen and read the poem.

Of a Statue Author: William

The statue cannot feel their eyes.

It cannot know they're really there.

No biting word can draw it's blood.

No hurtful glance can make it care.

The statue keeps its vigil there.

It watches with unseeing eyes,

It has no envy of the ones

Who scamper pointlessly around.

But then a pair of piercing eyes

Seek out the statue where it waits.

They gaze into its soul so still;

A stone tossed in the tranquil pond.

Hello there, says the pair of eyes,

What are you doing over here?

And would you like to join with us?

We've room for just one more, you see.

The statue slowly shakes its head,

And, setting loose the dust of years,

It makes an odd, uncertain sound

As if to say, you speak to me?

The pair of eyes will not relent,

And as they meet the statue's own

It sees that there's a face behind

The eyes; a face filled with concern.

The statue makes its mouth a smile

And says with manufactured strength,

I'm fine, I'm fine, don't bother me.

I just prefer it over here.

The eyes and face are satisfied,

Receding into their bright world.

They leave the statue quite perplexed,

Its point of view all broken up.

Perhaps there something to be said

For that that's called Humanity,

Perhaps its worth the pain for one

Who can't fit in to nonetheless

Still seek the bright society

Of those who fit in all to well;

To seek to see and to be seen

As human.

Because some of them care.

Noreen paused as she finished the poem and there was silence around the table as she gave the typers time to process. She placed a hand on Adam's shoulder.

Adam's IPAD was positioned in front of him on the table and he reached forward, leaning his forearm on the table and typed, "I FEEL LIKE THE PERSON IN THIS POEM COULD BE A METAPHOR FOR TYPING TO ME." Adam rested for a couple of seconds and then continued, "THE STATUE REALIZED THAT SOME HUMANS CARE. IT WAS AS IF BEFORE HE HAD THE INTERACTION WITH THAT ONE PERSON, HE FELT ALONE - LIKE NO ONE SAW HIM. THEN, FROM

THAT ONE INTERACTION, IT WAS LIKE A VEIL WAS LIFTED."

Adam paused again, smiled and then typed, "YET IN A FLEETING MOMENT, FROM A SOUL'S SINCERE EMBRACE, A VEIL OF ICY STILLNESS LIFTED, REVEALING WARMTH AND GRACE. IN THAT ONE TOUCH OF KINDNESS, HIS SOLITUDE WAS TORN, HE GLIMPSED A WORLD OF CARING, IN A NEW LIGHT REBORN.

"WHEN I STARTED TO TYPE IT WAS LIKE A VEIL WAS LIFTED FOR ME!"

Noreen smiled, "Always adding those poetic thoughts, Adam!" Over the years Noreen had noticed that the phrasing typers used came out very poetic, lyrical. Recently, she was supporting a typer, Kevin, who was one of three boys, all who had the autism diagnosis. While her client relied on typing to communicate, his brothers were able to speak words and Kevin's brother Ty came out with a doozy as they were discussing the right to communicate: "IF I HAVE A FUNCTIONING LARYNX OR SOME OTHER WAY TO COMMUNICATE, IT WOULD BE EASIER TO DIVERT A RIVER FROM ITS' COURSE THAN TO GET ME TO STOP TALKING. I NEED MY CONVERSANT TO BE AS DIRECT AS POSSIBLE. DANCING AROUND THE POINT WILL ONLY GET YOU AS FAR AS TRYING TO USE A SPOON TO TRAVEL UPRIVER. "

Noreen smiled at the memory, picturing paddling upriver with a spoon, then came back to the current discussion asking one of the other typers, "Chad, what do you think?"

Chad was a bit contrary. Frequently, it felt like he disagreed with whatever was being said just to ruffle feathers. But Chad paired his contrariness with a wicked sense of humor. He did not disappoint Noreen today.

"WHY DID THE STATUE GET SO EXCITED AFTER IT WAS FINALLY UNVEILED?" typed Chad with a slight grin. "HA, CHAD! OK. I'LL BITE. WHY?" Adam typed.

"BECAUSE IT WAS TIRED OF BEING IN THE STONE-COLD SHADOWS!" answered Chad and everyone giggled.

Gail stood next to Chad. Chad was independent with his typing - meaning that he no longer required touch to help his movement. He still needed help setting up his tablet, but didn't need the physical touch to type his thoughts.

For whatever reason, some folks still needed to have a support person close by. In individual sessions Chad had been working on having longer and longer distances with his support person, and had gotten to the point where they could be at the back of a room, maybe 20 feet away. But if they got any farther than that Chad started to lose his train of thought. Or so it seemed. He would stop mid-sentence or misspell words more. Noreen knew that the folks who suggested supported typing could be summed up as one big Ouija board phenomenon would just say this was because Chad was picking up on cues from Gail, or whomever his support person was that day. But what confused Noreen about this was that these same people accepted that most non speaking persons with autism were severely retarded, or intellectually impaired to go with the current language. So, by default somehow someone with severe cognitive challenges is able to pick up on subtle cues from someone across the room that tells them which of 26 letters to type. You would think if they truly believed this, they would be scrambling to research what was going on.

Noreen shrugged off her momentary frustration at the typing detractors. She couldn't dwell on it. It was what it was, and some day we would understand why this worked for so many people. She just kept on, knowing how important it was to the people she served.

They continued going back and forth discussing the article.

Each of the four appreciated the poem with Joey deciding that it was a little too sad for him. Joey shared that when he reads something sad it tends to stick in his brain for a few days, and he would rather be stuck on happy thoughts.

As Noreen packed her bag at the end of the session she proposed inviting a new member to the group. "I met this young boy, Jake, and his mom, Meg. They are just beginning their typing journey and I wanted to ask you guys if you'd be ok if I invited them to one of our groups. It would be a drive for them, but I think it would be good for Jake to get a sense from you guys what independence can look like, Plus, I think Jake would have fun with you guys. He has some good jokes!"

Checking in with the YES/NO cards, the group voted unanimously to invite Jake and his mom.

It was a little before one when Noreen headed back down the mountain. She loved her sessions with this group, but she was no fan of the traffic on her way home so aimed to leave by early afternoon so she would miss the afternoon rush hours, or at least it was less likely she would get stuck in a traffic jam.

As she pulled out of the driveway she thought back to Jake's typing yesterday, trying to puzzle through what he could have meant. Was there a conversation he had overheard about someone killing something? Maybe they were referring to hunting? Maybe they were using it in the hyperbolic sense, as in "I could kill him!" when irritated with someone. She was curious what they would find out tomorrow, and excited at the possibility that they might join her Wednesday group.

Noreen glanced in her rear view mirror. There was a green Honda trailing a bit behind her and for some reason Noreen felt a chill up her spine. Something felt off to her, but she couldn't put her finger on it. She pulled up to the stop sign and thought her brakes felt a little mushy. She would have to have her husband, Harvey, take it into the dealer and have it checked out.

As she pulled out onto CA-18, the state highway that went from San Bernardino up to Big Bear Lake Noreen again had that fluttery feeling in her stomach that something was wrong. The green Honda followed behind.

There was a bend in the highway a couple miles ahead and he planned on following Noreen to this point. Ideally, she will have lost control and careened down the mountain before that, but if not he planned on giving her a little help at just the right spot where she would have nowhere to go but off the mountain. He was already spending the money in his head.

Noreen drove a little slower than usual given that she had that weird feeling in her stomach and the brakes were a little mushy when she stopped at the stop sign. She pumped the brakes lightly and they seemed to respond but still didn't quite catch as quickly as she was used to. Or, was she imagining it?

Noreen had driven this road many times, so had a sense for its' twists and turns. She knew there was a hairpin turn coming up and she alternated between thinking she should pull over and call AAA and telling herself she was being a worry wart.

He inched a little closer to Noreen as she slowed down.

Could she sense something wrong with the brakes? Well, even if she did there was nothing she could do about it now. About a half a mile and they'd reach the curve and it would be goodbye to Noreen!

She saw the green Honda in her mirror. "I wish he would back off a little!" Noreen muttered to herself. Given that her brakes seemed to be acting weirdly and the Honda was so close, she worried he was going to hit her. As she went around the next corner she saw the runaway truck ramp and at the last minute decided to veer off onto the ramp.

The turn was coming up. He had driven it several times now in an attempt to know when was the best time to turn towards Noreen's car.

"One. Two. Three!" he counted after hitting the mile marker

34. In his practice runs he realized that once he hit mile 34 it was about three seconds going at 50 mph to get to the point where he would veer into Noreen. He counted as much to pump himself up for the kill as he did for the timing. He accelerated and turned his car to the right.

Just as he turned the car to the right Noreen veered off on the ramp and jerked the car back to the left in surprise. "Dagnabbit!" he cried out as he lost control and careened down the mountain.

Noreen's car slowly came to a stop and she breathed a sigh of relief. As she was heading up the ramp she had tested the brakes and the pedal pushed to the floor with no resistance. They weren't working! Boy, was she thankful for that truck ramp!

Expert Opinion

A Closer Look At ABA And More on Dyspraxia In Autism On The Question: Is ABA The Only Evidence-Based Therapy In Autism?

There is a lot of debate between professions as to optimal approaches to therapy treatments for persons with autism. Not surprisingly then, one of the most confusing things for parents of a child newly diagnosed with autism is navigating the options for treatment. There is a plethora of treatment options/packages available and, often, different advice is given depending on a professional's training and experience. Two of the most common treatment approaches are **Applied Behavior Analysis** (ABA and **Sensory Integration Therapy** (SIT. A Board Certified Behavior Analyst (BCBA would likely recommend doing intensive behavior analysis. An occupational therapist would likely recommend **sensory integration therapy**. While I have witnessed people from both of these professions argue the benefits of ABA or SIT, interestingly there are now some ABA therapists that say they also use SIT.

htttheyps:/ /www.halso use SIT.elpguide .org/mental-health/autism/helping-your- child-with-autism-thrive

https://circlecityaba.com/exploring-the-importance-of-sensory-integration-in-aba-therapy/#:~:text=Sensory%20integration%20therapy%20is%20a,communicate%2C%20and%20interact%20with%20others.

Schaaf, R.C., Benevides, T., Mailloux, Z. et al. An Intervention for Sensory Difficulties in Children with Autism: A Randomized Trial. J Autism Dev Disord 44, 1493–1506 (2014). https://doi.org/10.1007/s10803-013-1983-8

https://www.autismspeaks.org/applied-behavior-analysis

While there are many approaches, ABA has been able to promote themselves as the "gold standard" treatment for autism, though many have questioned the research this is based on.

Further, others have reservations about how ABA is applied in autism therapies and some autistic individuals have reported post traumatic stress symptoms following ABA therapy. And, some have criticized the marketing of ABA as the "go to therapy" for autism.

Applied Behavior Analysis is based on the science of learning and behavior. In autism treatment, behaviors are assessed based on what the observer determines is their cause. Behavior analysts looks at what they refer to as the "ABCs" of behavior, the **A** stands for antecedent and is what happens before the behavior happens, the **B** stands for the behavior, and the **C** for the consequence of the behavior, or what a person derives from that behavior. In autism ABA therapy, behaviors are frequently described using negative terms like attention-seeking, non- compliance, avoidance or escape. Treatment plans use reinforcement or punishment to change behavior. For example, a child might be reinforced for a "good" behavior by giving them M & Ms.

Some criticisms against ABA treatment for persons with autism have included: 1 The persons most often doing the therapy, registered behavior technicians (RBT have very limited training including very limited training specific to autism, 2 ABA has used punishment such as electric shock and spray bottles and 3 ABA dehumanizes people by using treatment similar to training a dog in a rote manner, though I would argue that the relationship piece, important in dog training, is largely ignored in ABA science. Beyond this, RBT's supervisors, Board Certified Behavior Analysts (BCBAs, are not required to take any neuroscience or neurology courses related to autism. I believe understanding the unique neurology of autism is key to developing appropriate therapies, or at the very least, understanding that the autistic "behaviors" we see are because brain connections are different in persons with autism. For example, because the U loops that process "in real time" **proprioception** are over represented but body maps are not well represented, a neurologic explanation for the brain based function of hand flapping may be to increase body awareness (see page 257, Chammi.

In discrete trial training (DTT, a specific ABA method, parts of an activity are repetitively practiced and rewarded. In 1987 Ole Ivar Lovaas published a paper on his work using behavior analysis to treat children with autism. Though some argued that there wasn't any way to determine the effects of the intervention due to: 1 How the study selected subjects; 2 How assignments were made to control groups and 3 How the study measured "success", applied behavior analysts have promoted themselves as the gold standard of treatments for persons with autism.

Lovaas, O. I. (1987). Behavioral treatment and normal educational and intellectual functioning in young autistic children. Journal of Consulting and Clinical Psychology, 55(1), 3–9. https://doi.org/10.1037/0022-006X.55.1.3

Though ABA has been successful in promoting themselves as the only evidence based treatment for autism, recent analyses indicate the quality of the research is limited. For example of all the research only 4% of the 770 studies reviewed had a control group or an appropriate control group, and over half of the studies had potential for bias towards positive results. This review suggests that ABA treatments need to be compared to other existing treatment methods. Though there are some studies, many have major flaws.

For example, when ABA researchers compared sensory integration therapy (SIT) to ABA, the Sensory Integration treatment was not conducted by a therapist trained and certified in SIT (Devlin et al 2011). Further, when I took a course in Applied Behavior Analysis in graduate school, I learned of a paper comparing SIT to ABA for treating the self-injurious behavior seen in autism (Mason & Iwata 2011). In this treatment study the SIT treatment protocol was to put a child in a room, alone, with a rocking chair that had a vibrating pillow on it; the room had flashing lights and a cassette recorder that played rock or jazz. Any occupational or physical therapist familiar with sensory integration would tell you this is a mockery of what sensory integration is.

Mason, S. A., & Iwata, B. A. (1990). Artifactual effects of sensory-integrative therapy on self-injurious behavior. Journal of   Applied Behavior Analysis, 23(3), 361-370.
Devlin, S., Healy, O., Leader, G., & Hughes, B. M. (2011). Comparison of behavioral intervention and sensory-integration therapy in the treatment of challenging behavior. Journal of autism and developmental disorders, 41, 1303-1320.

Opinion Based On Professional Experience:

While I do believe that applied behavior analysis has a place in autism treatment, I also think it can be harmful. Partially because direct care staff, who might only receive on the job training, and RBTs, who are limited to a 40 hour training that does not require education about autism specifically, are the ones that most often implement the treatments.

Another reason I believe it can be harmful is how it plays out in "real life" - I have found bordering on abusive. To illustrate from personal experience, a few years back I was consulting at an intermediate care facility - today's equivalent of institutions. One day I came into one of the houses and one of my non verbal autism clients, M, was on the floor, crying. She had thrown her shoes off. Standing next to her, ignoring M, was her one on one aide. I asked M what was going on and the aide told me to ignore it - M was just looking for attention.

"That is one way to look at it. You could also look at it that she is trying to communicate something." I responded. The aide ignored me as I looked closer at M and realized her shoes and socks were soaking wet. When I got

M dry socks and shoes, she stopped crying and calmed.

M's story might not seem like a big thing, but consider if you spent your life with an aide that interpreted crying as attention seeking and ignored you, as they were trained to do by ABA therapists - every day of your life. There is a reason why there are reports of PTSD from autistic individuals who have undergone intensive ABA therapy, and it's not solely from extreme measures like the electric shock treatments that have been used. Beyond M's story, there are reports of abuse and death from poorly trained staff.

https://www.wgbh.org/news/local/2023-09-11/electric-shock-therapy-is-still-allowed-in-one-mass-treatment-facility-advocates-say-change-is-long-overdue
Gitimoghaddam, M., Chichkine, N., McArthur, L., Sangha, S. S., & Symington, V. (2022). Applied behavior analysis in children and youth with autism spectrum disorders: a scoping review. Perspectives on behavior science, 45(3), 521-557.

Another challenge seen in ABA is what is referred to as prompt dependency. This happens when a person learns a task but can't initiate it on their own. For example, a child may learn how to say "Hi!" but can't initiate it unless their mom prompts them with, "Say hi Johnny!" An interesting relevant aside, I believe the neurology that underlies prompt dependency is also the neurology that underlies why persons with autism need the supports in typing, but also can be influenced by these supports, discussed further below.

On Communication Difficulties In ABA...

Several years ago now, I met an autism mom who is a behavior therapist as well as an occupational therapist and we were talking about the breakdown between ABA therapists and people in other fields. This mom shared with me that at the last ABA conference she had attended there was a breakout session called something like, "Why other fields hate us." It surprised me that they would have such a session at one of their conferences, but it made sense to me, given the interactions I had with many ABA therapists over the years.

In reviewing for this book, I came across a blog post titled *BCBAs are Ass**les (Sometimes)* written by a BCBA, "Inappropriate Opossum", who is also **neurodivergent.** While I wouldn't describe BCBAs as assh**es, I have had many a conversation with behaviorists that have left me feeling unheard and frustrated.

One example was when I met with two BCBAs who worked at the facility I was consulting with in an attempt to have more consistency with staff in-servicing and programming. I wanted them to understand where I was coming from, what I understood about the neurology of autism, but was met with mildly disguised derisive stares and tones. I have wondered if the reaction I have received from BCBAs when I bring up the neurology of autism is simply a result of their training. They have been taught that you can't interpret behavior from anything other than what you can observe. So when I bring up how different brain connectivity can result in different behaviors, I am told just that - you can't know what is going on in the brain. And then am largely ignored - I have wondered if they believe if they give me a punishment of sorts - if they respond negatively to my inviting them to lunch to discuss the neurology of autism, I won't ask again.

Another example, when I was taking the ABA course in grad school, the Professor used a video example of a young boy with autism who had difficulty sitting still to do his math assignment, "non-compliance behavior". The BCBA and the parents were working out a plan to improve this boy's time spent cooperatively on math. One thing that stood out to me was how they didn't include the boy in any of the discussion and it seemed to me that that would be the first thing you would want to do with any child, giving them agency to contribute to the therapy goals.

I asked the professor if they had included the child in on the collaboration and he said, "No." then paused for a minute, "While it may have been appropriate with this boy, other kids just wouldn't understand." Now, at the heart of my philosophy is that you can't know how much a person understands if they have motor challenges and can't speak. So, better to err on the side of assuming they understand, the least dangerous assumption, and speak with respect, assuming they understand everything you are saying. Though I have encountered some BCBAs who *do* talk to their clients respectfully, in in over thirty years of experience, I have found this is the exception not the rule.

There is a whole area of education research that examines what happens when a teacher has high, or low, expectations of students. It is called the Rosenthal or Pygmalion effect. An example of the Rosenthal effect, two teachers were assigned students at random, but one teacher was told they had the "slow learners" while the other teacher was told they had the "gifted students". Though the classes were equal in regards to their IQ initially, the classroom where the teacher was told the students were gifted did significantly better academically at the end of the year. I saw this effect when we went to Adam's Camp with my son, where he first typed.

Historically, special education programs have focused on where students fall short with little emphasis on strengths, and this was my experience as a parent with Kris. But, when we took Kris to Adam's camp, there was a real focus on emphasizing strengths. I noted how positively and respectfully the therapists interacted with Kris. I noticed how Kris seemed so much happier. I would pick him up at the end of the day and he would "talk" to me as best he could "Ah Choo choo. Ah choo choo." with the sounds he could make. It might sound like a cliche, but people really do know when you *believe* in them. Alternatively, people do know when you *doubt* their ability.

In contrast to how happy he was at camp that summer, earlier in the summer Kris had been attending summer school but he had a substitute rather than his regular teacher. A week or two into the program I noticed Kris did not want to get on the bus, and was crying a lot more. I decided to visit the school to check in with his teacher. When I arrived at the school Kris was out on the playground with a young man I did not know. This young man was a volunteer and was assigned to Kris as a one on one aide, without my knowledge. He did not know I was Kris' mom. I watched the young man interact with Kris and wasn't very fond of the gruffness I observed.

But it was what I observed a few minutes later when, during a musical chairs game in the classroom, the young man pushed Kris into a chair when the music stopped. Kris leaned forward slowly as if he might bite the young man. The young man exclaimed, "Did you see that? He tried to bite me!" Needless to say the young man did not understand what kind of supports a severely dyspraxic boy would need to play musical chairs, instead using force to have him sit. Also needless to say, I don't think Kris felt this young man believed in him.

Because of the assumption many have that non verbal children are severely retarded, and the structure of the science of ABA, I have often seen therapists talk negatively in front of children. For example, when I ask a child something, or comment to them, I have been told "He can't talk.", in a disparaging tone. Or, "Be careful keep a wide berth or he'll hit you!" when approaching an elderly gentleman with autism.

Neither of these comments was at all helpful. Imagine if you understood much more than you could express and understood these negative comments that happened daily.

Both of these comments spoke disparagingly about the people they were referring to. The first reminds the child of their communication difficulties - I have met *so* many typers who *so wish* they could talk. Beyond that, there was no reason to inform me this person couldn't talk. I knew that, but didn't feel it was any reason not to address them like a person. Common sense tells us it's just not respectful to talk about a person negatively in front of them. I would suspect that it would feel pretty cruddy to have someone talk about you in front of you when there isn't anything you want more than to be able to talk.

The second comment, while warning me of potential danger, was not at all helpful. What the staff didn't understand is that people with autism rely on external cues to navigate their environment, while also having a hard time breaking in and out of learned movement programs. For R, I assumed he had gotten into a pattern where he hit staff when he felt unsafe. So if staff primed his motor system to think of hitting someone, he was actually more likely to hit me than he would've been if the staff member hadn't said anything. The thought of hitting someone brought that motor program to mind, an external cue. Because R had a hard time controlling that motor program, the staff essentially made it more likely I would be hit than less likely.

To illustrate this a little more I want to talk about one of the developmental dyspraxia studies by Smith and Bryson that was published in 2007. In this study, they examined people with autism's ability to perform gestures but also looked at if people with autism could do nonsense movements with familiar tools. For example, if they held a toothbrush in their hands instead of pretending to brush

Smith, I. M., & Bryson, S. E. (2007). Gesture imitation in autism: II. Symbolic gestures and pantomimed object use. *Cognitive Neuropsychology, 24*(7), 679-700.

their teeth they would instead wave it three times above their head. People with autism have a particularly challenging time doing this and instead will do the conventional movement of brushing their teeth. In therapy we talk about that child being stuck in that pattern.

Similarly, in a separate study looking at motor learning profiles, Haswell and colleagues (2009) taught autistic participants to capture animals on a computer screen in a specific pattern with their arm and hand. Then they changed the paradigm so the participants had to use a different path that relied on their visuomotor system. The autistic participants had a hard time breaking out of the initial pattern indicating that they relied on the "internal model" of a movement rather than being able to adjust using the visuomotor system.

So what does this mean? Because people with autism have difficulties with imitation, and praxis more generally, they tend to get stuck in certain movement patterns or sequences that they have learned. In the Smith & Bryson study, autistic participants couldn't break out of the familiar gesture, such as they're brushing their teeth with a toothbrush, and wave it above their head. In R's case, he had gotten into a pattern of hitting when he felt unsafe[my interpretation]. *Because* his brain connections didn't allow for him to inhibit this, he would have a proportionately more difficult time stopping himself from inhibiting this.

Before I close on this, I want to go back to the staff telling me that the elderly gentleman, R, would hit me. I don't really blame him (the staff). He was just going with what he was taught, and the program was heavily reliant on ABA, which tends to negate the importance of the neurology of autism, instead interpreting autistic behavior in the same way we would someone with a typical nervous system. At the core of ABA, behavior is only evaluated with what we can observe. So, anything we also know neurologically about autism is not considered when developing treatment plans.

So with R, the staff did not understand about R's motor difficulties. The staff assumed he could do everything in the same way they could motor wise. So, as this staff explained, when they went to get R up out of bed, he didn't move so, believing he was just being resistant or "non compliant", they drug him out of bed. And, R hit him. Now, I did not see the staff get R out of bed, but I have seen others manhandle clients I have known with autism - grab them a little more forcefully than I was comfortable with, creating a feeling of unsafety for the autistic person - if you have difficulties with movement and someone attempts to move you, you might resist. Alternatively, for staff, understanding the motor challenges and how to use supports could kept the staff person safer as they would have approached R with entirely different expectations.

I believe that when you train direct staff, describing behaviors in negative ways, without understanding the underlying neurology and motor differences, can create a situation where any "inappropriate" behavior is looked at as volitional - totally under the autistic person's control. "He can, he just won't" e.g.

So, in the getting R out of bed example, the staff assumed that R had total control and was just being "non-compliant" with the request to get out of bed. But, had the staff understood that R had difficulty with motor initiation, and were trained with giving him proper supports like amplified proprioception and others, they might have not had to drag R out of bed, creating the situation where he felt unsafe and struck out. In the 30 minutes I had worked with R that day, he did not hit me when I worked with him, in close proximity, and stretched his legs, given good supports.

In Movement Differences and Diversity in Autism/Mental Retardation, Donnellan and Leary use a quote from a behaviorist to speak to the general "inhumaness" of how ABA is used in autism, using a quote from a behaviorist when attending a conference session on normalizing supports, "We have to humanize them before we can normalize them."

Perhaps because, inherent to ABA, is the concept that you have the power to change someone's behavior, this leads to a larger sense of the power one person has over another.

Decisions are often made without any input of the person receiving the treatment. Granted, if clients are limited in their ability to communicate, you might be hindered on getting any kind of feedback or input. But because you can't know how much any communication challenged client understands, I believe it is always best to explain your approach and to *always always* speak respectfully.

Inappropriate Opossum speaks to her ABA colleagues about the breakdown in communication between ABA therapists and other fields on a post about electric

Warning - this shows a child being shocked at the Rotenberg center shocks and punishments used in ABA:

It might come as no surprise that almost nothing we've been taught about the Judge Rottenberg Center, (JRC) is correct. The facts about them, all of the statements made in their defense, have become scripts parroted across the field like a religious litany. Indeed, the comparison to a religion is not used ironically. As social media amplifies criticism of ABA, the field has only become more and more closed in on itself and defensive. Of course there is a growing number learning and attempting to change the field, but there is also a frightening number banding together and clinging to these scripts like a security blanket.

 Now, I have never witnessed electric shock being used but the underlying mentality of having power to control someone else's behavior combined with a l ack of understanding of the neurology of the disorder has created a space where, at least some in the ABA field, believe electric shock is warranted to control behaviors. In one of the documentaries the above blog post mentions, one child was shocked when he let up on a switch. Now, I don't know the specifics of that incident, but what if that child was dyspraxic and had difficulty maintaining control, of the switch? As I have discussed, BCBA therapists or educators working from a behavioral model don't necessarily keep up with the motor learning and dyspraxia research, albeit this research is relatively new. I believe that working from the model that autism is a neurologic disorder that presents, at least partially, as developmental dyspraxia would

help all therapists better understand why certain supports work, but also why some behaviors are present. This would in turn better serve autistic persons.

Turning to Ole Lovaas, the father of ABA and autism, I wanted to share a comment he made in a 1974 interview with *Psychology Today*. Beyond Lovaas referring to children with autism as "little monsters", similar to the ABA person Donnellan and Leary quote, he says:

> You see, you start pretty much from scratch when you work with an autistic child. You have a person in the physical sense– they have hair, a nose, and a mouth– but they are not people in the psychological sense. One way to look at the job of helping autistic kids is to see it as a matter of constructing a person. You have the raw materials, but I/you have to build the person. One can easily see how this attitude could filter down within the discipline.

I want to close this section addressing positives of ABA. Though I have brought up many reasons why I feel like ABA therapy may be harmful to persons with autism, there are reasons I do think it can be beneficial. First, if you are teaching a new skill that will always be done the same way, like tying your shoes or buttoning your pants, the repetition and reward philosophy would be helpful, and it doesn't matter so much if the person gets stuck in this pattern. This doesn't work as well when teaching spoken words.

Further, we all use ABA principles - the ABCs of behavior, even if we don't know it. For example, if I am talking to someone (A) and they yawn and then look away, disinterested, I might realize they might not be interested in what I am saying.

My behavior (B), talking on a particular subject, produced a yawn and a look of disinterest, the consequence (C). So, I might not bring this subject up again with this person.

Any good therapist should take advantage of ABA principles, even if it is to sincerely say, "You did it! Good for you!" It's just when a child has neurologic differences resulting in communication and motor difficulties, it is really important to know the function and dysfunction of the neurologic areas affected. It is time all clinicians working for persons with autism have an understanding of the unique motor challenges that accompany autism. Next, let's look further at some of these neurologic differences.

Simple Movements, Developmental Motor Mapping And Voluntary Motor Control. How Might Developmental Dyspraxia Play Out In Children With Autism?

At first, movements in infants are thought to be reflexive in nature. The neural connections responsible for reflexes are present at birth. One example is the grasp reflex, a newborn grasps your finger if you put it in the palm of their hand. As infants grow and experience the world, new connections are formed in the brain, creating opportunities for voluntary movements. As young children are learning new movement skills and gestures, the movements are not refined at first, and the repetitive movements we see in autism we also see in typical infants and toddlers.

These repetitive movements are typically simpler movements such as leg kicking or arm waving. Or, you might notice a two year old banging a cup or spoon on the table repetitively. It is thought that as babies grow and are able to learn new, more complex motor skills, because of increased brain connections, these repetitive movements subside.

In order to be able to learn and perform new movements, one needs to have good brain connectivity, including good connections to "motor maps", called **homunculi,** in the brain.

All typical adult brains have maps in different parts of the brain. So if a neurosurgeon were to go into the sensory area of the brain and stimulate the "finger area" of the map, it would feel like someone was touching your finger. If the finger area of the motor map was stimulated, you would see your finger move. In infants, it is thought these  maps aren't fully formed until the infant experiences their environment. In fact, these maps can change throughout life. For example, if you started to learn the piano, the finger area would get larger and then smaller again as your ability improved and became automatic.

Watson, A. H. D. (2006). What can studying musicians tell us about motor control of the hand. Journal of anatomy, 208(4), 527-542.

The reason why I am discussing motor and sensory maps is that there is evidence that these maps are not well mapped out in persons with autism. There is also anatomical evidence that areas of the cerebellum are undeveloped - there are less neurons. Though we are still learning about the cerebellum, proprioception and movement are moderated by the cerebellum. The cerebellum fine tunes movements by comparing the location of where your body part is with where you are aiming it go. So, as a thought experiment, if the cerebellum is supposed to have 100 neurons, but it only has 10, the information from the body as it moves would not register correctly in the brain, thus maps might not be accurately formed. Consistent with this, one investigator, using movement analysis has demonstrated that the part of the proprioceptive system that processes "in real time" movement is corrupted.

Torres, E. B., Brincker, M., Isenhower, R. W., Yanovich, P., Stigler, K. A., Nurnberger, J. I. et al. (2013). Autism: the micro-movement perspective. *Frontiers in integrative neuroscience*, *7*, 32.

Proprioception is the body awareness sense, but you can also think of these brain pathways as fine tuning the speed and accuracy of movements. Have you ever misjudged how heavy an object is and picked it up too forcefully? This is because your brain, from prior experience, "knows" how much force to use given the estimation of weight.

But what would happen if you didn't have a strong mapping of how much or little force to use? Your brain never got the memo of how much muscle force is appropriate for a given action? It is conceivable you would see movements that are not in control.

And what would happen if you couldn't learn new, more complicated movements because the brain connections didn't form correctly that allowed you to copy movements? For one thing, you might get stuck with relying solely on repetitive, simple movements.

Miller M, Chukoskie L, Zinni M, Townsend J, Trauner D. Dyspraxia, motor function and visual-motor integration in autism. Behav Brain Res. 2014 Aug 1;269:95-102. doi: 10.1016/j.bbr.2014.04.011. Epub 2014 Apr 15. PMID: 24742861; PMCID: PMC4072207.

Müller, R. A., Pierce, K., Ambrose, J. B., Allen, G., & Courchesne, E. (2001). Atypical patterns of cerebral motor activation in autism: a functional magnetic resonance study. Biological psychiatry, 49(8), 665-676

Mostofsky SH, Ewen JB. Altered connectivity and action model formation in autism is autism. Neuroscientist. 2011 Aug;17(4):437-48. doi: 10.1177/1073858410392381. Epub 2011 Apr 5. PMID: 21467306; PMCID: PMC3974163.

Steinman KJ, Mostofsky SH, Denckla MB. Toward a narrower, more pragmatic view of developmental dyspraxia. J Child Neurol. 2010 Jan;25(1):71-81. doi: 10.1177/0883073809342591.

PMID: 20032517; PMCID: PMC2892896.

Another observation I have made over the years is that for many nonverbal children with autism, the accessible purposeful movements are "simpler". 

Whereas the typical child, shown first, would rotate her forearm as part of the scooping motion, the child with autism rotated much less and seemed to coincide with flexing and extending his wrist. I urge clinicians to look at this next time they are working with someone with autism. Not only to consider how an inefficiently connected praxis system could present, but also to consider challenges in teaching new motor skills.

Seeing simpler movements may indicate that the movement is coming more from the primary motor cortex as if we stimulate the primary motor cortex we tend to get simpler movements like flexing and extending your wrist. But, if the premotor area is stimulated, we tend to see more complex movements like bending the wrist as you rotate the forearm.

The premotor area is part of the visuomotor brain pathway. The visuomotor system is what we use to imitate movements, and to adjust our bodies as needed in order to catch a ball.

Many children with autism can learn to catch a ball, but if it goes outside their "target zone", and they need to adjust their body, they have a lot of difficulty.

Brain Motor Areas

One reason this is relevant is that the visuomotor pathway is not well connected in persons with autism. One academic group at Johns Hopkins that has been looking at movement differences has examined the visuomotor system:

> Our twice replicated findings confirm that visual-motor functional connectivity is disrupted in ASD. Furthermore, the observed temporal incongruity between visual and motor systems, which may reflect diminished integration of visual consequences with motor output, was predictive of the severity of social deficits and may contribute to impaired social-

communicative skill development in children with ASD.

Nebel MB, Eloyan A, Nettles CA, Sweeney KL, Ament K, Ward RE, Choe AS, Barber AD, Pekar JJ, Mostofsky SH. Intrinsic Visual-Motor Synchrony Correlates With Social Deficits in Autism. Biol Psychiatry. 2016 Apr 15;79(8):633-41. doi: 10.1016/j.biopsych.2015.08.029. Epub 2015 Sep 3. PMID: 26543004; PMCID: PMC4777671.

The visuomotor pathway starts in the back part of the brain then goes to the premotor cortex before going to the primary motor cortex. Because there is a disruption in this pathway, skills like learning new movements or breaking out of patterns of learned movements can be difficult. On the latter, an illustrative example might be if someone learns to hit a tennis ball with a racquet, they can do it as long as the movement stays in the exact pattern or to their "target zone" but if there is a body adjustment that needs to be made because the ball goes off to the right, they can't make the adjustment.

Glen's New Plan

If this were a cartoon, steam would be shooting out of Glen's ears. He had just gotten off the phone with his contact and learned that, for the second time now, the target was alive and the guy sent to kill her was dead. It reminded Glen of a joke about the incompetent musician. Something about he got locked out because he couldn't find the right key.

Glen ruffled some papers on his desk. His contact had given him a deal on a new team that was supposed to be much better. And, more expensive. But since the first guys were such idiots, he was able to get the second team at a discount. Glen realized how ridiculous that sounded, like a money back guarantee for hit men, and shook his head at the thought.

"Come on in!" Glen barked as he heard a knock on his door.

Tiffany, one of his board certified behavior analysts or BCBAs if you used the common acronym, came through the door. "Morning!" she chirped in a fake sincere way.

Glen got along well with Tiffany. Probably because she was almost as cynical as he was about the kids and families they worked with.

"How are things going out there?" Glen asked.

Tiffany rolled her eyes. "Well, that OT came in again. We got into a disagreement on neuroplasticity." Tiffany rolled her eyes again and continued. "I mean do they really think that sitting a kid in a swing will change his brain?"

"Can't be any more likely with those drums they use." Glen laughed, referring to a drumming technique some of their itinerant music therapists used to encourage eye movement. Glen made a gesture was if he was hitting a drum, his hand and arm shaking back and forth as he imitated a discoordinated movement.

In a mocking manner, Tiffany mimicked the movement, pretending to hit a drum while looking in the opposite direction. "Ooops! I missed, but watch how I can type words miraculously!" They both laughed.

"Seriously, things seem to be going ok. Andy had a melt down, which brought on a whole other discussion with the OT about what the melt down meant. She doesn't get ABA - she kept saying he was trying to tell us something. 'Yeah, I said - he's looking for our attention and to escape - so ignore him. He's trying to tell us he doesn't want to work!"

In autism therapies, there was more than the usual scientific debate. It got downright nasty sometimes. While occupational and physical therapists thought that you could build on the strengths of the child and work on building new brain pathways, behavior analysts looked at what a behavior might be telling you from the outside.

When it came to autism, the behaviors were described with words like escape behavior or non-compliance. They thought the only way you could interpret a behavior was what you could observe. You couldn't interpret it from a brain basis as we didn't really know what was happening there. So, if a child, Andy for example, was crying an ABA professional would say they were looking for attention - it was attention-seeking behavior. On the other hand, an OT or PT might say the child was trying to communicate something. The OT or PT might go on to say, "Yes, he's looking for attention because he is trying to tell you something!"

What Tiffany failed to tell Glen was that the OT also found that Andy's shoes were soaking wet from a puddle he had jumped in at recess and once the OT got dry socks and shoes from Andy's backpack, he settled and was fine. Communication or attention-seeking. I'll let the reader be the judge.

Getting back to business, Tiffany gave a nervous clearing of her throat. She knew Glen hated the regional center staff, "The regional center folks are coming for a visit this afternoon, so you'll need to sit down with them for a bit to go over paperwork." The regional center was an organization that had offices in counties throughout California and who managed medicaid monies for those with developmental disabilities. The Behavior Center's budget was about 75% regional center funding. Glen would have to put on his big boy pants and pull out the charm. Especially now - he couldn't have any red flags hold up funding. And, there were some red flags with Glen's double dipping, but thankfully they would be looking at records from six months ago.

Glen let out a big sigh. "Ok. I'll put on my big boy pants and schmooze them!"

"They should be here right about two." Tiffany smiled. "I'll let you know when they arrive. Do you want me to pick up some of those cupcakes you like?" Tiffany didn't really like Glen, heck - she didn't like most people. But she did know how to suck up, and she knew Glen loved red velvet cupcakes.

"That'd be great." Glen said and then shooed her away with his hand. He had forgotten about the regional center visit. He had some work to do to make sure the paperwork was in order, and he also had an important phone call to make.

June in Irvine California. There was a reason there was a song about it never raining in California. The sun hit hard when Glen opened the back door to the clinic, and Glen's transition glasses darkened in that creepy way, making his outward appearance a closer match to his insides.

Glen glanced out at the playground and noticed Jake was there again along with his buddy, Nick. Nick had a service dog, a golden retriever named Bear. Predictably, Glen was no fan of service dogs. He hated dogs - always barking, shedding or wanting attention. Now there was a law where they had to be let in public places. Sure, once in awhile he heard a story about a dog doing something for a child, but on the whole he thought it was a bunch of BS.

Jake and Nick hung out near each other in the yard. The clinic had an automatic bubble blower that staff had set up for them and Nick and Jake jumped up and down, laughing, and batted their hands at the bubbles. Jake wasn't sure why bubbles were so soothing, but they were. Maybe it was the sensory experience when they popped, or maybe popping bubbles was just a fun physical activity that he was able to do. He saw the bubble. He popped the bubble. Could it have anything to do with his movement being tied to external cues in the world like Noreen talked about? Jake didn't know. Nor did he care in this moment. He was just enjoying being in the sunshine with Nick and Bear, gleefully jumping and popping the bubbles.

Out of the corner of his eye, Jake saw someone come out of the clinic back door. He stopped jumping and stood silent when he noticed it was Dr. Glen. He really didn't like that guy. Jake walked over to an area of the playground where there was an oversized version of scrabble and picked up the letters B A D and placed them on the ground in front of the big board.

Nick and Bear watched, and after a moment Nick walked over and picked up the letters M A N and placed them next to Jake's word. There was a moment's pause then they both, almost in unison, broke out in laughter. It wasn't really funny, but in that moment they both saw the typer in each other, and that made them happy. The fact that they could share the thought about Glen, that they could share something with meaning and understanding, was huge and it was if it reached in and found the happy laughing place in their hearts.

After more than a minute of Jake and Nick bending over in belly laughs the laughter faded and Jake glanced over to where Glen was standing on the other side of the fence, holding a phone to his ear. He could make out some of what was being said. "Daisy Fudge, Noreen Schack…" Glen listed off five names.

Though Jake couldn't hear great, his ear pricked up when he heard the name Daisy. And then Noreen and some other names Jake didn't know. Noreen? thought Jake. How did Dr Donovan know Noreen? Was it the same Noreen? It was certainly an unusual name, but how could Glen know Noreen? Daisy? Was that the same Daisy Noreen was talking about? Jake heard a low growl come from Bear. Bear never growled.

The New Guys

Tony and Vito typically met for breakfast at the Eleven City Diner in the South Loop. They liked that they served breakfast all day and the ambience went back in time. The owners played hits from the 40s like *Boogie Woogie Bugle Boy* or *I'll be seeing you*. Ironically, though Tony and Vito's job duties included killing people for hire, they could be surprisingly sentimental.

Tony slipped into the diner booth, "Hey, Vito, you ever think about taking a vacation?"

Taking a sip of coffee, Vito replied, "A vacation? From what, the "thrill of the chase"?"

"Yeah, something like that. Maybe a nice beach, some sun.

Relax a bit." Tony gestured toward the sky.

"Sure, if you call "relaxing" hiding from the feds and avoiding our boss's next big plan. Sounds like paradise to me." Vito chuckled.

Tony grinned. "Maybe. I hear Hawaii's nice this time of year.

Plenty of places to hide a body!"

"It's not like we've run out of places around here…", countered Vito.

"True. But you gotta admit, the idea of trading in our suits for Hawaiian shirts does have a certain appeal."

"True, and we could even use our "surfboards" as getaway vehicles if things go sideways."

Tony laughed, "Fair point. Hey, speaking of getaways, remember that time we tried to use a hot air balloon?"

"Oh yeah. You almost took out half the city's power grid with that thing. That was one for the books!"

Tony grinned. "I'm still waiting for the city to send us a thank you note for giving them an extra-long blackout. Maybe they'll name a street after us: "Tony and Vito Lane.""

"We can put up a sign: "Slow down, or you'll end up with a big surprise.""

"Just don't put that on the resume. "Specializing in high-altitude escapes and unexpected blackouts.""

"And don't forget "expert in unintended fireworks displays." Just our luck, we'd end up in the newspaper for that." Vito grimaced, remembering the time Tony had loaded up the back of his pickup with fireworks then promptly forgot when he threw a match after lighting a cigarette and it flew into the pickup bed. Vito was impressed and thought it approached the fourth of July in Washington D.C. firework display. Tony, on the other hand, was not happy with the $2500 fine he had to pay.

"Ah, newspapers. The only time we get bad press is when someone forgets to follow the rules. Remember the "be quiet" rule?" Tony shook his head.

"Yeah, you and your loud hobbies. Maybe you should stick to knitting, Tony. It's quieter."

Tony, claiming mock offense, "Hey, my knitting's top-notch.

You should see the scarves I make. They're to die for!"

They both laughed heartily. "What did you order?" Tony asked as he picked up the menu.

Vito rolled his eyes. "Why do you ask? You order the same thing every time!"

"Well," Tony started but the ringing of his cell phone interrupted him.

"Hello? Tony here." He greeted the caller. Glen hesitated on the other end of the line. "Hello?" Tony repeated.

"Hi. Sam Manconi gave me your number. He told me to tell you the passphrase: Remember. Fireworks explode!"

Tony hated that passphrase but Sam thought it was hysterical, and Sam made the rules.

"Ok. What do you have for me?" Asked Tony.

"I have a few jobs for the button man." Button man was the term that Sam suggested he use.

"Hold on a minute. I'll be right with you." Tony gestured to Vito that he needed to go out back, and slipped out of the booth.

Tony leaned against the brick wall and spoke into the phone. "Ok, for security, I want you to give me a couple of the first names, then I'll have you email me the rest of the details."

You wouldn't know it from the banter he had with Vito in the diner, but Tony got down to business went it was time to get down to business, and his manner had switched from friendly banter to assertive professionalism. "Hold on a minute so I can take the names down."

Tony set the phone down and searched for the note cards and pen he kept in his pockets for just this reason. "Ok. I got it."

From the other end of the line, Glen said, "The first one is Daisy. Do you need to know where they are?"

"No." replied Tony. "Just the first names. You can tell me everything else in the email you send. And, to let you know, everything is secure. This is a burner phone."

"Ok." Glen acknowledged, "The second name is Noreen." Tony shared the email address and security details, having

Glen repeat the address and instructions back twice to assure accuracy. "You won't hear back from me. If we need to talk to you for any reason, Sam will reach out with communication details." Tony paused. "Got it?"

"Got it." answered Glen and they hung up their phones.

Back at the clinic as Glen hung up his phone, he noticed Jake and Nick sitting quietly in the padded asphalt of the playground. Bear lay between them staring intently at him. As their eyes met, Bear let out a low growl.

Jake Spills The Beans

Noreen and Meg had arranged with Nick's mom, Michelle, to have a two hour combined typing session. Noreen thought it might be regulating for Jake to have another typer as they talked through things. Jake and Meg had arrived a little early and they sat in the car while they waited. Raffi's greatest hits played over the speakers. It was one of Jake's favorites, but he wasn't listening. Instead, he was focusing hard on how he would tell Noreen that she was in danger.

Ever since Jake had learned about their gathering, he'd been strategizing on the best way for him to be able to tell Noreen and his mom about what he had overheard Glen say on his phone call. He thought about the way his brain processed whole words. It was like his brain took a screenshot of whatever he was seeing, sometimes it made sense, sometimes it did not.

Typically, if he saw a word, and you could figure out how that word was used, given the context it was used in, he could generally use it when he was typing. That is, in the limited time he had been typing.

He figured out if he practiced what he wanted to say and how he wanted to say it ahead of time, it was easier to control his body when he typed - it was more automatic. So he considered how and what to say and had been practicing that for the last 24 hours.

As the last song finished on the Raffi album, Meg turned off the car and collected her purse. She briefly reflected on how Jake seemed more quiet and focused than usual in the last couple days. Their last session with Noreen had stuck in her head and she had puzzled over what Jake meant when he had typed KILL. Meg finally came to the conclusion that someone made an angry remark around Jake, possibly about someone Jake liked, where they had use the word kill as in I could kill them! Thinking that relieved her mind some. But, Meg was in for a big shock later that afternoon.

Nick and Michelle were in the waiting room as Jake and Meg entered the clinic. Nick held a necklace of red beads, similar to the ones they gave out at New Orleans Mardi Gras, sporadically jangling the beads. Funnily, of all the autistic kids Meg had met since Jake was diagnosed, Nick was one of several kids she had met that used those beads to help them stay regulated. They just had different interactions with the beads. While Jake would slap his hands over them commonly letting out one of his EE sounds, Nick tended to just hold the beads and shake them.

Noreen usually liked going out to a park or café when she had groups of folks. Partially because it was just nice to have a change of scene, but mostly because she like to be out in the community - too often these guys were segregated from the rest of the world. But with Nick and Jake today, she decided to stay in the clinic. They were both fairly new to the typing, and Jake was very dysregulated the other day.

As such, Noreen guided them back to a room that was set up just for this purpose. Noreen had chosen comfy padded dining room chairs for this room. She wanted it to look and feel more inviting. And, of course, the chairs were straight backed with no arms so it made it easier to support folks when the were typing.

Noreen attended to Jake and Nick, pretty much ignoring Meg and Michelle. They didn't mind as they both sensed, and very much appreciated, how Noreen's manner seemed to calm their sons. For Bear, there was a dog bed in the corner nearest to where Nick sat. As more and more of their clients got service dogs, Noreen realized they needed to accommodate them too. She knew a lot of folks in the general public were dubious about the role of service dogs, but she was convinced it was a huge support for families after one mom shared with her a story about losing her son at the airport after he ran off into the terminal.

Five minutes later that mom saw her son walking back towards her, his hand resting on the golden retriever's back. Elopement, when a child ran off, was a huge worry for many families with autism and Noreen thought this was a great example of how service dogs were important for her folks. Either way, Bear smiled up at her, wagging his tail in appreciation for the cozy bed.

"So, I wanted to get started doing some of the S2C typing. By just reading a paragraph or two and then asking questions. It takes the pressure off, or at least some of the emotional pressure, and makes getting the movement easier."

Noreen had picked out a couple paragraphs from a book she was reading about how emotions affected the motor system. As she read, the words appeared on a screen on one side of the room, situated so that both Jake and Nick could follow along visually. Noreen had noted early on that when she combined the auditory and visual when reading, it seemed to help her folks process better. They seemed to be able to remember the word better.

"The emotional motor system is a fascinating aspect of human neurobiology that intertwines emotional experiences with physical responses. This system encompasses the neural pathways that connect emotional centers of the brain, such as the amygdala and the prefrontal cortex, to motor regions responsible for facial expressions, body movements, and vocalizations. For instance, when we experience joy, the emotional motor system activates facial muscles to produce a smile and may trigger a spontaneous, enthusiastic gesture.

Similarly, when faced with fear, this system can cause the body to adopt a defensive posture or induce a startle reflex. These responses are not merely reflexive but are deeply integrated with our subjective experience of emotions, allowing us to communicate our feelings to others in a visceral, non-verbal manner.

This emotional-motor connection is crucial for social interactions and empathy. By mirroring emotional expressions, people can better understand and relate to each other's feelings, fostering emotional bonds and effective communication. The synchronization between emotional experience and motor expression also plays a role in emotional regulation; for example, consciously practicing facial expressions associated with positive emotions can sometimes help shift our emotional state. This bidirectional relationship between feeling and expressing emotions underscores the complex interplay between mind and body, revealing how deeply our physiological responses are embedded within our emotional experiences."

It was a little more scientifically complex than she usually chose, but given that Jake had such a hard time the other day, she decided to go for it - sometimes just thinking about something complex could be regulating. When she reached words she thought might be unfamiliar to the boys, she would stop and spell it out. "Amygdala. A. M. Y. G. D. A. L. A."

"Ok. So, I chose this passage to read based on my experience with clients and how their emotions can affect their movements. I think this happened with you the other day, Jake." Noreen explained. "The first question I wanted to ask you guys is a simple yes/no answer. Do you feel that emotions affect how you move? Well, it may be a three answer question - maybe you're not sure."

Noreen had put the stencil boards in front of Meg and Michelle and she gestured for them to pick them up. "Ok guys, do you think emotions affect how you're able to move?"

Meg and Michelle picked up the boards and held them vertically in front of their respective sons, as Noreen had shown them. Next, they handed their sons a pencil. Noreen said this was the prompt to help them initiate the movement.

Jake took the pencil and typed YES and came out with one of his "AAHHH!" sounds as he finished typing the S.

Nick took the pencil and type NOT SURE.

"Ok." said Noreen, "So Nick is feeling like he's not sure if emotions control his body. Jake sounded like that was a pretty firm yes from you. Let's do one more question and then we'll move onto some words and then progress and we'll do some some other communication."

"Is the amygdala part of the emotional motor system?" Noreen asked next.

Both Nick and Jake chose yes this time. "OK so you both agreed with that. The next question I want you to type out. What did the article say that we could do to change our emotions?"

Slowly, but with determination, Jake typed out "make a funny face."

Nick typed, " Move like the emotion".

"Right! They essentially said to move your facial muscles in a way that showed the emotion you wanted to connect with".

Noreen commented. "So probably for most people that means making a funny face because at least for most people they prefer to channel happy than sad or mad."

She went on to praise the moms. Noreen was really impressed with how both moms were doing given that they had just started. "And good work Michelle and Meg! You guys seem to have a knack for this!"

"Ok. So let's talk a little more. Jake, it seemed like you were trying to tell us something when we had to end our session the other day. Nick, I asked your mom and Jake's mom if it was ok if we talked about it when you were here and Jake shared that he preferred that." Noreen wasn't 100 % sure, but it seemed like Nick sat up a little straighter when she said that. These guys could have difficulty with their emotional motor systems, but they responded to praise just like anyone else. Noreen thought it probably made Nick feel good that Jake would want him there.

"Let's readjust things so I can support you Jake." Noreen and Meg switched places and Noreen held the letter board and sat on Jake's right side. When supporting someone with resistance, it was easiest for the support person to sit on the same side as the person's handedness. In this case, Jake was right handed.

After settling into her chair and positioning things, Noreen asked, "What do you want to say Jake?", and offered her hand to Jake. This was not the time to work on independence. This was the time to help Jake get out what he wanted, almost needed, to say.

Jake stayed quiet in his chair today but reached for Noreen's hand and typed clearly, and with no emotion today, HE IS TRYING TO KILL YOU AND DAISY!

The room was silent for a moment then, keeping her voice calm and matter of fact, Noreen asked, "Who is trying to kill me Jake?"

Jake had taken a picture of the name in his head several times, but he wasn't really sure how it was spelled. GLEN DONAVAN.

This stopped Noreen in her tracks. Noreen thought back to her date with him once way back when. More recently, she had had several negative interactions with him over social media before she realized it was better to just let it go than take the bait.

"How do you know this, Jake?" asked Noreen. "PLAYGROUND. WITH NICK AND BEAR." Jake typed.

Noreen turned to Nick at this point, "Is that what you heard Nick?"

"YES." chose Nick when his mom offered the YES/NO cards. "Is there more you want to say?" Noreen asked Jake.

Jake typed, "THAT'S ALL I KNOW."

As Noreen sat there she thought about her brakes and the car that went off the side of the mountain. "Could that have been intentional?" Noreen thought, but decided not to share it with the group in this moment.

"Well, to say the least, I'm not really sure what to do with this information, but Jake I promise you I will be careful." Noreen paused. "And I promise you we will figure out what Dr. Glen meant." Noreen put the Dr. in front of Glen's name out of respect. She didn't like him, but he was well respected in the ABA field, and had a PhD. So, Noreen showed him respect.

She couldn't fathom that he would literally be trying to kill her, but the scene on the mountain road from a couple of days ago kept coming back into her mind's eye. Her gut told her it was something more than Jake overhearing a conversation where someone used the word kill when angry about something. While her thinking brain said "No way!" at the thought that someone would try and kill her, her gut countered, "Yes way!"

How was she going to figure this out?

A Call To Action

That same night Noreen arranged for a group zoom call with Meg, Kate, Michelle and their kids and husbands. Noreen stayed in that night and made sure her doors were locked, and the alarm was on. Years ago Harvey had bought her a gun as he was traveling a lot for work. Noreen absolutely despised guns, but she went ahead and took lessons at Harvey's insistent prodding and actually enjoyed it.

Noreen didn't really hate guns per se - her dad and brothers had hunted. More in the sense that in this country too many people had guns that shouldn't have guns. None of that mattered to Noreen in this moment - she was happy to have the security of the loaded gun in her nightstand as she slept.

Harvey had been home when she returned after her session and Noreen shared what had happened at the clinic.

"Do you think Glen Donovan could really want me killed?" Noreen looked at Harvey, staring at him with perplexity.

Harvey stared back at her, equally mystified. The idea that someone would actually hire a hit man out of the confines of the mob was unbelievable. But for anyone to try to kill Noreen?

Everyone loved Noreen! Harvey had heard stories from her about some of the more visible folks in the supported typing groups receiving death threats, but he figured it was all talk.

"Well, while it certainly sounds far-fetched, Gary did say that he couldn't rule out that someone messed with your brakes.

And, you did see the guy go over the cliff on your way home from Big Bear." Harvey paused thoughtfully. "Better safe than sorry. I think we should call the police."

Noreen met his eyes and shrugged, "I guess. I'm just not sure how much they will be able to do with the little evidence we have."

After further discussion, they did eventually call the police, but the sergeant they spoke with said there was nothing they could do at this point. He didn't even suggest the police stop by. So, they made sure they locked the doors, turned the alarm on and put the gun in the nightstand.

Not surprisingly, Noreen didn't sleep well that night. She kept having dreams of someone trying to "get her". So, it took her a bit to wake up the next morning. Harvey, as was his way when he was home, brought her coffee. Harvey was off today and had canceled his morning plans so he could be in on the zoom call.

Harvey sat on the side of the bed as Noreen drank her coffee. "Ya know, I have worried all these years that getting involved with the supported typing stuff would ruin your career, but I never in a million years would have thought it could actually be dangerous for you." Harvey reached forward and rubbed Noreen's shoulder.

"Me neither." agreed Noreen and took a deep breath. "I remember some of those death threats Daisy and Kevin received in the first couple of years. If anyone had asked me I would have said it's just talk, but there has been such acidity and..." Noreen paused, searching for the best word, "just downright meanness over the years from well-respected people who I would have never believed could possibly say such things. So…" Noreen stopped shrugged her shoulders, tilting her head. "So who knows?"

Later that day Noreen and Harvey had arrived at the clinic and met up with Jake, Meg, Nick, Michelle and Bear. Noreen situated everyone back in the room where they had had their last typing session. Pulling the connection link up on her computer and connecting it to the projector, Noreen shared with the group, "Ok. So I invited Adam and Kate as we have become close over the years and Kate was concerned. Plus, Adam's dad is big into technology and Kate thought he might be able to help us figure out a good strategy."

Signing into their virtual meeting, Kate and Adam appeared on the screen with a man, Adam's dad, Jerry. "Hi everyone!" Kate saluted.

"Kate, Adam and Jerry, let me introduce you to Jake, Nick, Meg, Michelle and my husband, Harvey." Noreen paused then added, "Oh - and I can't forget Bear! You can't see him but he's Nick's service dog hanging out with us in his dog bed."

"NOREEN, WHAT HAPPENS WHEN A HIT MAN FALLS ASLEEP?" Adam pushed the speak button on his communication app and it spoke his pre-typed words."

Noreen smiled and Harvey laughed. Harvey had met Adam before and heard many of his jokes through Noreen. "I have no idea Adam, what?"

"HE GOES UNDERCOVER!" Adam replied laughing.

Noreen waited for the laughter to dissipate before saying, "Well, thanks for beginning with some comedic humor Adam. We could use it as the subject of this meeting is pretty dark."

"Yeah, this has got to be the weirdest meeting I think I ever will attend." Harvey said.

"I'll second that!" Jerry chimed in. "Can you tell us what you know Noreen?"

"Well, Jake and Nick are the ones who know best, but I'll sum it up. As you all know, Glen Donovan has dedicated a large portion of his career to bashing supported typing." Noreen paused and took a deep breath. "I can't fathom that he would want to kill someone over this, but the events of the last couple of weeks gives me lots of pause."

The group nodded their heads in agreement, and Noreen continued. "First, I spoke with Daisy last night as she is one of the names Jake and Nick overheard. After I shared what I knew, Daisy told me that a few weeks back she was on the metro platform and someone fell off the platform. She couldn't be sure, but she did wonder for a brief second if he was trying to push her, and now was reconsidering again. I wouldn't have known about it had I not called her as she hadn't thought of it but for a brief moment.

"Second, last week as I was driving back from Big Bear, my brakes were feeling odd - mushy. There was a car behind me and I was worried about them possibly failing so I took the runaway truck ramp, which was good because my brakes really did fail!"

Kate interrupted in a worried tone, "Why didn't you call us?"

"I totally appreciate the concern, I didn't want to worry or stress you guys. The police drove me to the station and Harvey picked me up there so I was all set.

"But the other thing was that, out of the corner of my eye, the car that was following me seemed to swerve towards me just as I swerved onto the truck ramp. He ended up swerving right off the mountain."

Jake cried out "Ahhhh!"

"I agree Jake, pretty crazy, huh?" Noreen acknowledged. "On the one hand, it happened. On the other hand, it feels so crazy."

"So, you had no reason to think you'd been targeted?" asked Jerry.

"No, not really. I mean I had one of those weird gut feelings like something was wrong, but chalked it up to the issue with the brakes." Noreen answered.

"The third thing is that Jake shared that he heard Glen Donovan when he was out on the playground. First, by himself, and then again with Nick and Bear."

"What did they hear?" Kate asked, a very concerned look creasing her face.

Noreen turned to Jake and Nick, "Do you guys want to tell them?"

Similar to Adam, Jake and his mom had preprogrammed his communication device after discussing it with Noreen. Noreen thought that if Jake was ok with it, it was best for him to tell his part of the story.

"THE FIRST DAY GLEN SAID, I JUST WANT THEM DEAD! THE SECOND DAY WITH NICK, WE HEARD HIM REFER TO DAISY, NOREEN AND OTHERS."

Confirming with Nick, Noreen asked. "Just to confirm Nick, is that what you heard?"

Michelle supported Nick to type "YES!"

"I have to say this is beyond ironic - that Glen could be found out by the very individuals using a method he has been so critical of for so many years. I mean ironic in a good way - so way to go Jake and Nick!" Kate commented.

The group sat for a moment, soaking in what Jake and Nick had shared. "So now what do we do?" asked Meg, rubbing Jake on his back. "I have to admit I'm a more than a little daunted." Again, everyone was silent for another moment.

"I don't know but Noreen took the gun out of the safe last night for the first time in years and let me put it in the nightstand. She might not admit it to you guys, but she is scared." Harvey looked around the room and at the camera lens at everyone. "And that means I'm scared too."

Crazy scary." Kate chimed in and turned to Jerry. "I think Jerry has some ideas."

"I'm not sure if you all are aware, but one of my hobbies is investigating new technology and one of the things I'm into is listening devices." Jerry told the group. "There's all kinds of them out there right now and I think there's one we could put on the playground to record when it hears a voice. We would probably hear a lot of kid talk, but since Jake and Nick have now heard two separate conversation, it makes sense that Glen might go out to the playground again to communicate with whomever he's talking to. Meg, could you have Jake show you where he was? I think the fact that you work at the clinic and Jake goes there is going to help a lot."

"Of course." Meg agreed. We can do it next time we're at the clinic."

Jerry continued. "Great. The other tech option we can use is an app we can put on his computer that will record and transmit what is happening on Glen's computers. I think this may be the better bet in terms of the information we get, but I say we go at it with all guns loaded. We can also put a nanny cam type thing behind his desk so that we can see what password he uses on his computer and any other conversation he has in his office. What do you guys think?" Jerry asked the group.

Noreen met Harvey's look of dismay with one of her own. "Aside from this all still sounding so crazy, I think it just may be doable - if it's easy enough to hide the devices."

"They're pretty small. I'm a little worried about the playground one though but I can go help Meg one night if we agree this is the way to go."

"I'd feel better if we did that." said Noreen. "I'm a little worried Meg and Jake might get caught. It would probably go quicker if you were there with them when we put the devices in."

"Ok. I can just say I'm a friend who came to drop off a serving tray she left at our last get together, or something like that." Jerry proposed.

"Good idea!" Kate agreed, "You can do that right after you clean out the garage!" They all laughed, including Jerry. He was fully aware how much Kate did for their home and tried to make up for it in other ways, like helping implant listening devices at a therapy clinic, for example.

"Ok, team. Sounds like we have a plan!" Noreen said, in an attempt to remain upbeat and end the meeting..

But Kate added one more thing, in a somber tone. "Noreen, I know we are all kind of in a shock state - not really believing that this could be possible, but please, please be careful. I would never get over it if something happened to you."

Again, the room was silent, Meg looking into Noreen's eyes through the camera lens.

"I'm working from home until this is all sorted out. So, Noreen is stuck with me until that time." Harvey told the group.

"Good." agreed the group and they signed off.

Listening In

Meg arrived at the clinic a little later than usual that night to assure she wouldn't run into anyone at the clinic. She and Jerry had made arrangements for him to arrive a little later so that Meg would have time to get some cleaning done and make sure no one was there.

Jake, unusually quiet, understood the stakes of getting the devices in place. Maybe more than anyone, as he heard Glen's tone on the phone. While the adults in the group still seemed to have some doubt Glen really wanted to kill Noreen, Jake knew he was serious.

Jake and Meg had gotten in a rhythm with his typing since he was able to share about Glen with them. Since talking to his mom and Noreen about Glen he had been able to control his body better. He had been thinking about it a lot since he had the discussion about emotions controlling his body.

Sitting in one of the bean bags in what the staff called the sensory room, Jake had a favorite show playing on his tablet. But he wasn't really paying attention. Instead, he was thinking over the past couple of weeks and how many changes had come into his life. He felt like a part of him had woken up since meeting Noreen and beginning typing - like the things he was learning through Noreen about his brain allowed him to understand why he did certain things and then he could navigate things better. Like when he practiced what he was going to say about Glen in his head. He never would have thought of that before learning about Noreen's theory of how his brain captures words. It all made sense to him when he thought about how words seemed to float around in his brain. Now, he knew.

In terms of the emotional motor control, as Noreen referred to it, it was like big emotions either helped him do something or totally sabotaged it. The physical relaxation he felt once he was able to share what Glen had said was remarkable to him. He had never been able to share anything that complex and emotionally charged. Granted, this was particularly emotionally charged, but there were other things that were emotionally charged in different ways. Like the time he witnessed two staff being abusive with one of his cohorts who had had a dysregulation incident and pulled one staff's hair.

They had put Billy in a room where Jake had been sitting on a break and started shouting at him and pushing him. One time they even pulled his hair, "See - how does this feel? Doesn't feel good does it?"

Jake was able to not have a melt-down, as a lot of the staff called it, in that moment but it hung on with him for a long while. And, now that he understood emotional motor better, Jake thought that because he wasn't able to tell anyone, he had more than a few "meltdowns", including pulling his mom's hair a couple times. He hated himself when he did that, which just added to the emotional overload. Jake felt a sense of relief wash over him as he again realized that now he had a way to get at least some of his emotions out.

Meg peaked through the door. "Hey Jake, Jerry is here so we're going to head back to the playground to hide the device."

Jake looked up at her, stood up and moved through the clinic with Meg. Meg was mildly amazed at how easily he was able to get himself up and walked with her. Amazed because a month ago it would have taken several attempts before he was able to get his body up. Mildly, because she had already gotten fairly used to Jake being more…. she searched for the right word.

Regulated. Regulated in the sense that he seemed to be having less melt downs and when she asked him to do something, like walk to the playground, he was able to do it with less prompting.

Jerry was waiting for them out back. "Jake communicated Glen was standing over in this area." Meg pointed to a back corner of the playground fence.

"Let's see where we can put it unobtrusively." Jerry suggested and walked to that area.

It took a little bit of searching and thinking before they found a spot that would work. There was a drainage ditch that was covered by a grate and Jerry hid it away using some neoprene material and duct tape. Meg was really glad he was there - she didn't think she would have been able to figure that out, or at least not in the short time that Jerry was able to.

Luckily, it took Jerry even less time to put the app on Glen's computer. Luckily because just as Jerry finished they heard keys jingling in the front door lock. Jerry put his finger to his lips at Meg and Jake and pointed to a closet door.

Debating momentarily whether to make an excuse for being there or hiding, Jerry stepped inside and closed the door.

Meg glancing around the room trying to think of what to do, spotted a cleaning bottle and wipe she had left earlier. Swiftly picking it up, sprayed a shelf and started wiping.

"Jake, what should we do tomorrow?" Meg asked, trying to maintain a matter-of-fact tone as Glen walked through his office door.

"You're here later than usual." Glen remarked, taken off balance for a minute.

"Jake and I had a social group we were attending this afternoon, so I thought no one would mind if I came a little later." explained Meg.

Glen paused, intently looking between Meg and Jake.

Reasonable, but for some reason it didn't sit right in his belly - it felt off. He easily shook it off quickly - unsurprisingly, Glen's intuitive sense was anything but finely honed. He had too many dark thoughts ruling his world.

"I was doing some work at home and forgot a file." Glen said as he walked over to a filing cabinet and brought out his keys. It was notable to Meg because Glen rarely locked any drawers. For a long time Meg thought it was just because he was the absent- minded professor type. Now she wondered if he was just too arrogant to think anyone would dare go through his office.

Either way, the fact that Glen would start locking his drawers now seemed remarkable.

"Fascinating, but scary. Looks like he has something to hide." she thought.

"Tiffany said you've been doing that typing stuff with Jake." Glen said in a derisive tone.

To say the least neither Jake nor Meg appreciated his tone.

Meg made sure to keep her irritation in check though. "We have. It's been pretty eye-opening, and well, just plain awesome."

"You do know there is nothing more than a Ouija board phenomenon with that stuff. It's all what the person supporting sees." Glen said condescendingly.

Meg took a deep breath before she spoke next. "Have you ever met any of the individuals that have become independent after needing support for a long time? Have you ever met any of those same folks that can read their words? Have you ever felt what the movement is like?" She knew it was probably best to not challenge him, but she couldn't stop herself in the moment.

Ignoring a direct answer to her questions, Glen hesitated then sputtered a bit. "Lots of kids with autism can read words without really knowing what they are saying. It's called hyperlexia. That means a person can read words but has no idea what they mean."

Meg started to consider how to answer his comment but Glen turned and looked at the closet, seeming to consider something. "Well, it's all a bunch of bull." Glen added as he started towards the closet.

Meg asked louder than was necessary so that Jerry could hear. "What do you need in the closet?" and then abruptly bumped her leg into a table hitting her shin so hard it hurt for real. "OWW!!" She cried out loudly in an attempt to distract Glen from opening the closet.

Realizing what she was doing, Jake joined in, putting his hand to his mouth similar to when folks, disrespectfully, imitated an Indian war cry the sound "OOooOOoo" that an American Indian might make, only Jake's sounded with an a vowel. "WAHwahWAHwah."

Their impromptu strategy worked and Glen turned away from the closet and turned his attention to them. "You ok?"

"OW!" Meg repeated and sat in a chair rubbing her shin. "I think I'll be ok - just being a klutz and will probably have a big bruise. Can I help you find something?"

"No. I just needed to grab some files." Seeming to forget the closet in the moment, he turned back to the filing cabinet, unlocked it and grabbed a couple of files after rifling through the cabinet for a minute.

"Ok." Meg continued rubbing her shin and Jake had quieted.

Closing and locking the filing cabinet, Glen turned and took the couple steps to the closet and opened the door. At this point all Jake and Meg could do was hold their breath in silence. Glen stepped into the oversized closet, grabbed a box of pens from the shelf and turned and closed the door. There was no sign of Jerry, and Meg let out a huge, audible, sigh of relief. "Where is he?" she thought.

Glen turned to her as he heard her. "You sure you're ok?"

Meg smiled, genuinely, because they had been successful at planting the devices and Jerry had escaped detection. They did it! "Yes, I'll be fine."

Glen turned to walk out and then looked back at his computer then briefly at Meg, seeming to judge if it was safe to leave there with Meg and Jake. Making his decision, Glen walked over, unplugged his laptop and placed it under his arm.

"You really should consider staying away from this whole supported typing stuff." Glen couldn't help himself.

Meg paused as if to consider for a moment. "I'll take your advice into account." Though, of course, she had absolutely no intention of doing so.

"Well, don't come calling me if you land yourself in prison." Glen remarked cryptically.

"O.K." Meg said in a monotone voice, trying to keep the condescension out of her tone, somewhat successfully. Glen turned and gave her a sideways look but didn't say anything. Instead, he turned and walked out of the room.

It was a good couple of minutes after Glen closed and locked the front door before anyone said anything. Hearing Glen's car pull out of the lot, Meg opened the closet door. "He's gone, Jerry." she cried out. "You can come out now!"

A door Meg hadn't noticed at the back of the closet opened and Jerry emerged. "Yeesh! That was a close call!" And they all broke out in uncontrolled, post-anxiety laughter.

"Can you believe how smug he is?" asked Meg. "Did you hear what he said to me? Using his words: What an imbecile!"

"He is most definitely an imbecile." Jerry agreed. Jake too, though all he could get out was an "Ahh!"

"I heard you ask what he was needing in the closet, and thankfully saw the door at the back. That was definitely a close one, but we did it. And, thank god we got the app on the computer before he took it." Jerry said glancing at the desk.

"Thank god." agreed Meg. "I totally had the heebie jeebies being in the same room with him. How about you Jake?"

Meg walked over to Jake, choosing to offer him the agree/disagree cards she had made up on index cards so she could have them ready in her back pocket at a moment's notice. Jake chose "AGREE" and came out with a new sound "AG" in a guttural tone. Meg had noticed that since starting typing, Jake had started coming out with different intonations and sounds with his verbalizations. This time it sounded like he was trying to say the word agree.

When they arrived at their respective homes later that evening they all felt a mixture of relief, but no one in their group slept well. They knew this was far from over. Jerry had a glass of wine with Kate and told her all about it. Meg and Jake stopped at McDonald's and Meg ordered a large french fry for Jake and a milkshake for her. Later, at home, they curled up and watched Forest Gump, Jake fell asleep midway.

Expert Opinion

Miscellaneous Observations On Typing Over The Years

Challenges with testing . When Kris first typed with me it was only one word, but the context combined with the feel of him pushing forward to the board with his finger extended was very clear. No one could convince me that in that moment the communication was coming anywhere but from Kris. On the other hand, I am confident there is no way he could have sat through, much less pass, a testing situation like the set up in the O.D. Heck study at that point - his body was too dysregulated and I would guess there were some words he wouldn't know how to type. But, that doesn't mean he didn't learn how to spell RAFFI and recognize the alphabet.

Beyond lack of knowledge on spelling words or dysregulation, I have found there is variance in how typers interact with the written word. Some automatically read words when they see them and have difficulty *not* automatically reading them. So, when designing an experiment it would be difficult to have written instructions as these readers might not be able to see a word and type it without saying it out loud.

Some typers have low-tone more relaxed bodies. Some have almost ballistic automatic repetitive movements.

Some are farther along the road to becoming independent. The type (shoulder, hand, wrist or handing a pencil) and amount of support (heavy resistance vs a light touch; amount of verbal and rhythmic cues etc.) varies greatly between these individuals.

Some typers are easily able to follow with their eyes. Some have oculomotor apraxia or similar conditions that affect voluntary eye movements.

Some appear to have relatively good visuomotor skills - they can easily follow a moving target or reach towards a moving object. Many others aren't able to reach for a large handle on a door.

I have found clear communication over the years, when typing with a new typer, when they clearly have been exposed/ know the word and they are very motivated to type with you. I have also had moments, especially early on, where I didn't get any communication.

There are numerous reports of beginning typers only typing with certain people, and frequently new typers have difficulty when typing with their parents. My best guess given my personal experience, is that every parent child relationship has its own patterns, and people with autism can get really stuck in patterns. It's like you have to adjust to a whole new way of communicating. I knew after Kris typed with me that he knew how to spell the word Raffi, but I have no idea if he knew how to spell "Could you take me to get some french fries?" He'd seen and heard Raffi hundreds of times, and knew his ABCs (he had watched Wheel of Fortune numerous times), but did he know how to spell french fries?

Clinicians have found that slight adjustments in body mechanics can greatly influence responses - whether there is a clear response, no response or misspellings. In many of the studies that show clear influence there are a variety of visual and auditory blocks used, which may have impacted body mechanics (Below, picture from OD Heck study).

This is the main reason I returned to graduate school - to understand the neurologic basis for why we (supported typing proponents) see communication but when under the blind set ups there was such strong influence - see *The neurology of typing,* pg. 249.

2000-2010 New Documentaries And Criticisms

In 2001 the documentary Autism is a World came out. This documentary is about a young woman,

Sue Rubin, who learns to type using facilitated communication and is able to attend college. Sue still has autism and needs support, but she types on her own on  a keyboard. One detractor doesn't remark on how cool it is  that she is able to communicate, but instead claims Sue Rubin didn't really have "simply autism", she really had a chromosome abnormality and that her autism was milder, despite Sue's fascination with spoons, echolalic language and head banging . No explanation - just that the documentary doesn't address the influence studies and she implies that even if this was true, Sue didn't have "true" autism. There are many disabilities and genetic disorders that are associated with autism.

2005 Pat Mirenda and David Beukelman publish Augmentative and alternative communication - supporting children and adults with complex communication needs and include a pro- FC statement:

> In regard to small group of people around the world who began communicating through FC (facilitated communication) and are now able to type either independently or with minimal hand on shoulder support... There could be no doubt that, for them, (facilitated communication) 'worked', in that open the

door to communication for the first time… For them, the controversy has ended. (And Mirenda 19 898, page 327.; Beukelman & Mirenda 2005, pg. 326.)

It is important to note that Mirenda later retracted her statement. Now, I do not know exactly why Mirenda changed her mind. I have wondered, based on personal experience in grad school (see pg. 240), if she publicly changed her mind, at least in part, due to the controversy and how it might affect her career.

Also in 2005, *Autism and the Myth of the Person Alone* became available to purchase. Sticking to his qualitative research training, Biklen collaborates with six autistic typers - each of whom had become independent with their typing after a lengthy period of needing physical support. In a personal conversation with a colleague, I was told that the facilitated communication institute decided to move towards supporting people to become independent. This book has chapters detailing typer's experiences with typing.

A review left on the book illustrates the break down of communication between different 'factions':

I am now going to do something very reluctantly-- write a review in response to another review, without actually reading the book. That's because the topic is so important, and reliable research has already been done. I have a friend with an autistic child so I have watched for any evidence supporting FC with great interest.

Basically, double-blind research studies into "Facilitated Communication" have found that whatever is typed is NOT a communication from the autistic person, but rather coming from the expectations of the facilitator.

Scientifically speaking, FC is only controversial because some people are so attached to the idea of it working that they are ignoring the research.

Ignoring the research? This reviewer didn't even read the book! My point is that this book *was* research. Sure, the studies evidence influence, but there is more to the story that Biklen, in his qualitative work, is trying to demonstrate.

Katharine Beals, an academic who has a PhD in linguistics, says she has switched gears and now teaches autism at Drexel University. Katharine Beals reviewed *Autism and the Myth of the Person Alone* and essentially discounts all of Biklen's book as she states because of "authorship issues" (these people were independent with accessing the keyboard when placed in front of them), the contributors on the book should be called 'subjects' not contributors.

Beals has a blog on a website that gives a very negatively biased view, in my opinion. In a recent communication with me, Beals states "We've looked at everything there is on (purported) apraxia and motor disorders in autism." Yet, she was unfamiliar with the two praxis and visuomotor learning papers I sent her, chosen fairly randomly out of hundreds of choices) to illustrate the motor differences. Even though multiple respected academics have identified motor difficulties in persons with autism, Beals and her colleagues continually point to no evidence of motor difficulties. How can someone present themselves as an autism expert on a blog, frequently using comments such as: 1) How proponents of Facilitated Communication describe autism as a "purported motor disorder," or, 2) Why apraxia cannot possibly explain supported typing, yet remain unfamiliar with the latest motor research?

Beals does address what praxis is and how a disorder of praxis presents, but relies on quotes from websites rather than having any expertise. Now, I would not expect her to be a motor learning expert, but I would at least expect her to be familiar with the recent research if she is *teaching* college students about autism. Interestingly, on the contributors section of her website it says that many of the contributors have been directly affected by FC abuse allegations. So, maybe that is part of the passion behind Beal's assertions rather than basing her opinions on the whole of scientific research.

September 2006. Accepted into the Cognitive and Behavioral Neuroscience area of Psychology at the University of Florida, Kathy Berger, this author, returns to school at the age of 44, hoping to understand and explain the neurological underpinnings to questions like "Why would someone need resistance in order to initiate a movement? Or, why did I clearly have communication with Kris and yet there is strong evidence for influence?

In her first semester at the University of Florida, Daniel Wegner is invited to give a talk on his paper, "Clever Hands: Uncontrolled Intelligence in Facilitated Communication." In this paper, Wegner set up a study designed to assess why it is that facilitators don't think they are influencing communication when they are. Wegner rejects the **ideomotor** effect, an effect that happens when muscles may activate anticipating a certain action. For example, when golfers imagine making a putt, we may see activation of "putting" muscles on an EMG recording, without movement. Wegner rejected this, saying this phenomenon doesn't sustain.

Further, he proposed, confusingly, and without neurologic justification, that the influence isn't noted by the support person because somehow their nervous system is misled or subverted. "[in the ideomotor effect] the processes that usually accompany action production and simultaneously operate to ascertain authorship (so to indicate that the action is authored by the self) are subverted or misled such that the source of the action becomes unclear. This approach, then, depends on the idea that people are not perfectly informed of their authorship by the processes by which their voluntary action is produced. Rather, the determination of authorship is an add-on, a judgment reached through the perception of self and situation rather than through some privileged understanding that arises from the conscious causation of the action".

In a series of experiments with people with no neurologic differences, he attempted to explain the influence seen in FC. Basically, Wegner attempted to show that facilitators could influence even when they weren't aware they were.

When he finished I walked up to him and asked "So, if there is influence, what should we do with these guys?" He suggested to wait until they were independent. I shook my head and walked away, but wondered to myself how he thought we should support them to *become* independent?

The Email

Jerry rolled out of bed at five the next morning, careful not to wake Kate.. He'd been tossing and turning for the last two hours and finally threw in the towel. He was itching to get things set up so they could monitor Glen's computer and the nanny cam they had hidden between the books on Glen's bookshelf behind his desk.

Carrying his morning coffee, Jerry sat behind his desk in his home office. The windows were open as it was a bright sunny day and the temperature had yet to warm up for the day. As Jerry worked, he listened to the birds chirping in the garden. He realized he loved this time of morning. He would have to make more of an effort to rise and shine as they say. As Jerry loved his time to himself late at night, he usually slept in. Kate, on the other hand was early to bed and early to rise, though she seemed to be sleeping pretty soundly. The events of the past couple days must have caught up with her, he thought.

Jerry started up the computer and took a sip of coffee, pondering again the night before, chills running up his spine. They had come so close to being caught!

As he waited for the computer to boot up, he thought back to the first time he typed with Adam. While Kate was much more optimistic in the beginning, when she first told him about the supported typing stuff, he was skeptical, to say the least.

Statistics was his major in college, and he was very much a numbers crunching type of guy. That is, he really believed in the scientific method. What Adam showed him the first time he typed with him was that you couldn't make assumptions about the world, and what we knew through science was but one factor when evaluating things. Sometimes, we simply just didn't know yet - we didn't have the right tools to measure things; or we interpreted studies incorrectly; or sometimes, more like most times, egos got in the way. Regarding supported typing, most of the prominent researchers in this area had started and spent most of their years in autism research assuming kids who had autism who couldn't speak were mentally retarded. In keeping with his love of science, Jerry was at first angry when Kate talk to him about the supported typing and he looked it up on the internet. Most of the sites warned against using the technique, saying it was a discredited technique that could be dangerous.

Even some professional organizations warned against using the method.

But he bent to Kate's direction and kept his mouth shut. The first time he typed with Jake, he had gotten out some ABC overlays for the touch and tell educational toy Kate had been working with Adam on. He told Adam he was a little doubtful but this therapist said he knew his ABCs so let's give it a try.

Jerry resisted Adam's arm moving forward to the touch and tell device like Noreen and Kate had shown him, his eyes widening in astonishment as Adam forcefully pushed against his hand, while sitting quiet and engaged.

Adam knew all of his ABC's! He got a little confused with upper and lowercase but, there was no doubt in Jerry's mind at that point that Adam knew his ABC's. It was really no wonder, given that Adam love to watch wheel of Fortune and Disney sing- along videos that had the closed captions. Strangely, Jerry hadn't considered that Adam saw the letters announced every night on Wheel of Fortune - it had become part of their nighttime routine.

The computer dinged, bringing Jerry back to the present. He first checked his email for anything that came in overnight.

Jerry was the head of the I.T. department at a local university. He enjoyed it for the most part, but he didn't enjoy interacting with folks when they were frustrated because their computer wasn't doing what they needed it to do. But it was great in terms of flexibility - like he was able to work from home right now.

After helping a couple of frustrated souls out with their technology, he turned to the app that was recording Glen's emails. It looked like Glen had written three emails the night before.

The first two were quick replies to colleagues about some question they had. He froze a little when he read the third one though.

Tony and Vito,

I am glad I was finally able to get the correct email. As requested, I am sending along the names and locations of the people I want you to kill. The first is a woman in Melbourne, Australia, Daisy Fudge. The second is a woman in Los Angeles, California, Noreen Schack. The third is a woman who lives in Alexandria, Virginia Judy

Ascension. Last is a woman in Dallas, Texas. Her name is Umi Toma.

I can wire the first quarter of the payment to your account as soon as I receive the bank details.

Please let me know any other questions you have.

Best,

Glen Donovan

The emails went back and forth a couple times after Donovan's initial message. Tony and Vito gave their bank details and asked for any insights Donovan had for a good time for Noreen.

Jerry sat absorbed as much for what it was as who it was.

That is, he had never thought much about how it worked to hire a hit man, so it was fascinating to read. He wondered how much Glen had to come up with to pay them. How much did a hit man cost? He wondered how Glen was able to get ahold of them. The whole thing felt so insane - it was insane.

After calling Noreen and telling her, Jerry sent a text to their group chat they had started with all of the folks at their virtual meeting. *They* didn't need to worry about someone trying to spy on them.

Hey guys,

I just read a couple of email exchanges between Glen and a couple of guys - Vito and Tony (can you believe the names)? Anyways, the gist is that Glen did indeed hire a couple of hit men, and Noreen's name is on the list. I suggest we get on another meeting and talk next steps.

Let's all stay where we are though, I think that's the safest plan.

I say the sooner the better, Does that work for you all? Let me know and I'll send out a link.

This is Jerry if you didn't have me saved in contacts.

Jerry walked out on the patio while he waited to hear back from everyone. They had invested in a high quality outdoor seating system and Kate loved to garden so their back yard was like a little oasis.

As Jerry sat down in his favorite rocker, Kate poked her head through the open sliding glass door, "Morning honey. I saw your text. Oh my goodness!"

"I know. Crazy. Insane. I have no other words." Jerry agreed.

Kate sat next to Jerry and placed her hand on his leg. "Should we call the police again?"

"I don't know. Feels like we should, but the reaction we got last time doesn't give me much hope that they'll do anything, and we might get in trouble if we shared the information we have.

They might let him know. We can see what the group says, but I'm thinking we should wait until we know more." Jerry said and covered her hand with his own.

They sat in silence for a few minutes, looking out at the yard sipping their coffees. The bing of multiple texts coming through brought them back to the present moment.

"Ok. Everyone is good to meet in an hour. I'm gonna go send out a Zoom link." Jerry squeezed Kate's hand and headed back to his office."

The Entrapment

The group met virtually, each in their respective homes, sans Nick and Michelle as they were at an appointment. No one had slept well the previous night. Of course, Jerry and Kate didn't sleep well. Ditto for Noreen and Harvey. Noreen and Harvey stayed up late watching West Wing, one of their favorite shows. Much to Jake and Megs delight, Noreen ended up getting up and turned on Forest Gump, one of her favorites too, and they didn't fall asleep again until 4 am. Needless to say, they were all a little tired except for Adam, who was blissfully unaware of what happened at the clinic the night before.

Jerry started the meeting, "Hey everyone. So, I think everyone had the gist of what Meg, Jake and I experienced last night? It was a real suspense thriller!"

Meg laughed. "I think Jake and I almost swallowed our hearts when Glen went in the closet- not in the loving way, in the slamming our hearts into our throats way."

Kate brought her hand to her heart and shook her head. "I don't know about anyone else, but I am still having a hard time wrapping my head around this even though we now have clear confirmation Glen Donovan wants to kill Noreen and not only Noreen. Have you spoken with Daisy, Noreen?"

"Yes. She is having a hard time believing it as well, but is being careful. I think I told you all, but a couple of weeks ago Daisy was taking the metro home and a guy fell on the tracks. Thinking back on it she realized right before he fell she had bent down to tie her shoes. The police had said this guy was part of the Honoured Society, an organization similar to the mob in Australia. After I told her about Jake's communication and my mountain incident she thought back to the guy falling off the platform and put it in a different light. Always seeing the bright side of things Daisy commented on how she was lucky to have ADHD. If she hadn't missed tying her shoes, he might not have missed!"

The group laughed a little at the thought of being thankful for having ADHD then Harvey proposed a question. "The thing I keep coming back to is how in the world can Glen feel so much hate for someone like Noreen that he seeks out a hit man? I just don't get it."

"I'm thinking given who he is after and knowing his views on supported typing, that it comes down to that. It sounds crazy to me, but the debate has been truly awful over the years, with many passionate, and at times hateful, voices. Still, I'm in full agreement with you Jerry. I can't wrap my mind around the fact that anyone, much less someone in an industry that serves those with development disabilities would be so ..." Noreen searched for the right word, "unbelievably awful."

"I guess it's like any mental heath issue. We can't see it, so have a harder time understanding it if we haven't experienced it. I have a friend who has had depression bouts on and off over the years after the death of her son. There are times when she just can't motivate. I don't get it. I just want to get her up and go do something, but she just can't. It's like the motivation part of her brain just died. Her brain changed." Noreen paused. "Maybe it's the same with people who hire hit men.. I guess it must be like the part of their brain that cares about other people just died."

Kate joined in. "That makes sense to me. I've found over the years that my belief that at heart all people are good is not necessarily the best assumption to have when dealing with people. Maybe mostly because those same people don't believe what I believe - that people are basically good. They have a different belief system - one built around them. While *I* may think that authentically apologizing if I've done something wrong is all you need to do to move forward in a relationship I have had many friends who just can't apologize. I find I get stuck in these relationships."

Kate continued. "I've found some people could care less and feel like that apology is just their invitation to pile on and tell you how horrible you are . I found while I really like to be kind, some people don't. And they're not really interested in changing. I'm guessing Glen is one of those. I'm not sure what happened to him early on in life to make him that way, but I'm thinking he definitely, doesn't care about being kind."

Jake seemed to have something to say. And Noreen brought out the letter board. Jake typed, " CLINIC HAS MEAN STAFF."

Each of the adults furrowed their brows, wondering what Jake was referring to. A pit in each of their stomachs.

"Can you explain that further Jake?" Noreen asked gently. "Ahhh." verbalized Jake and he reached toward the keyboard again. "HIT AND YELLED AT BILLY. MARK AND SZY."

"I'm so sorry you had to go through that Jake. It's never OK to be mean. After we figure out and stop Glen, we'll work on reporting that to Medicaid and the regional centers." Noreen assured Jake.

"We totally will!" agreed Jerry.

Finishing a communication while they talked, Adam pushed the talk button on his device. "MY EXPERIENCE WITH ABA WAS DOTTED WITH A LOT OF ROTTEN-EGG STORIES . IN THE OLD DAYS THEY USED TO FLICK THEIR FINGERS AT OUR FACE OR LOCKED US IN CLOSETS IN THE DARK. IT WAS SCARY. W   E NEED TO LOCK DR. GLEN UP!"

Jake vocalized his "Ahhs" and Meg, taking his cue, supported him to type. "YES! LOCK HIM UP!"

"OK. So it appears we are all in agreement that Glen should be locked up. What's going on in your head Noreen?" Harvey said, noticing a thoughtful look on Noreen's face.

"What I have often wondered is why the detractors of supported typing don't try it with someone. Why wouldn't they want to fully understand? Sure, the studies done in the 90s showed influence, but the interpretation seems to be that influence is *all* that is happening. Certainly, we know that's wrong."

On a roll, Noreen continued, "I've puzzled over this for a long time. I just don't understand how the people who bash supported typing so much don't try and understand it more. It's like once those studies showed the influence that's all that has been focused on. I mean, why don't they go try and support someone communicating with typing? Why don't they try and feel what the resistance is like? Why don't they seek out those who are now independent and try to learn from them? It would seem to me if I was really opposed to something, I'd wanna understand exactly what it was what I'm against."

Harvey picked up the thread. "There's a speech given by a Warren Buffett colleague, Charlie Munger, that talks about the psychology of human misjudgments. He talks about things in science and how they move so slowly. Some of it he equates to these academic folks getting so honed in on what they are studying, besides, having such big egos, that they get to the point where they just can't hear anyone who offers a differing viewpoint. He tells this story about a law professor at Harvard that got so full of himself and his ideas that his colleagues ridiculed him for thinking that declarative judgements equated to curing cancer. In other words, he was so full of exaggerated ego that he didn't, well actually couldn't comprehend that everyone else wasn't equally enamored with his ideas."

Jerry, who had a few start and stops in graduate school since starting his career, snorted. "I've met a few of those folks!"

Harvey laughed and continued. "He talks about the man with the hammer syndrome where when you get come up with ideas that have a profound impact, you tend to use that idea, that hammer, if you will, for any problem you come across. I think folks who use ABA with autism have that a bit. While we all use behavioral principles, ABA with autism tends to neglect that it is a neurologic condition. Of course, we all do it in that we rely on things we know that work. When it becomes a problem when a person gets so enamored with that idea that the fail to think anyone else could have a better idea."

Harvey paused, took a drink of water and smiled. "I could go on for hours, but I promise, this is my last point. Another point he made that I think makes sense here is that there is what he refers to as commitment and consistency bias. So when new ideas or theories come out and point in a different direction, folks who have built their careers on the old theories can't let go of their previous conclusions. He talks about Max Plank and how when the new physics came out it wasn't until younger academics took over, academics who didn't have the entrenched mindset, did the new physics take hold."

"So, hundreds if not thousands of people with autism aren't able to access communication as richly as they could, rather than simply using PECS to request, because some old man sitting in an ivory tower doesn't want to admit he's wrong?" Meg jumped into the conversation.

"Unfortunately, yes. Or at least if you agree with what Charles is saying. I think about my experience with academia. It's such a cutthroat environment in many ways, but it falls very short on the ideal what science should be." Harvey shrugged. "Too many big egos obsessed with their own ideas. Some psychiatrist might call it narcissism. But either way, Glen certainly seems to have some bias!"

"Yeah. It's not just with the typing stuff. I remember many conversations with behavior therapists and others over the years about sensory integration techniques and neuroplasticity and having them openly laugh at me at the idea that you could change your brain based on what your experience is." Noreen put her hand to her forehead and shook her head in disbelief. "If you google neuroplasticity in scholar google you come up with over 200,000 hits! And this research started way back in the sixties so it's not like it hasn't been around for awhile!"

Adam started typing something and the group waited until he could finish. Meg had noticed there was a whole different rhythm to timing when you were having a conversation with typers as it took them time to type out their thoughts. But the group was used to this and so as soon as they all noticed Adam typing, they paused out of respect.

"DR. GLEN MAY HAVE WANDERED THROUGH LIFE'S VAST EXPANSE NEVER TOUCHED BY LOVE'S GENTLE EMBRACE."

Adam's communication device spoke his typed words.

"Always the poet, Adam. Agreed. I'm educated guessing that Dr. Glen has not experienced a lot of love in his life. I often wonder if we had a way of turning up the 'love volume' for folks what the world would look like." Kate responded.

"A LOT BETTER!" Typed Adam. "Agreed!" The group confirmed.

"Ok. Not that I am not totally fascinated with this discussion but we'd better get to what we need to do for this present moment." Harvey said, looking around the room for tacit agreement.

Finding that agreement, Harvey continued, his voice grim. "So, we now have confirmed, crazily enough, that Donovan is indeed talking to a couple of hit men about killing Noreen as well as Daisy, Judy and Umi. And, it sounds like Noreen may be first on the list."

"I say we need to do something proactive at this point. Make a plan so we can control things." Jerry said. "Or at least have more control." He added.

"I've been thinking about it and I was wondering if there was some way we could set it up where Glen thinks that Noreen will be alone at her office or something, and we arrange for the police to be there." Harvey proposed.

"I'm not sure the police will come after our last interaction?" Meg countered.

"Maybe. Maybe not. We'll have to take that into consideration." Jerry said. "I think Harvey has a good idea. We need to set something up so we can control it. Meg, what's the chance you could arrange to have Donovan over hear a conversation you have with Noreen?"

Meg thought about it for a few seconds, stroking her pony tail as she thought. "I think I could do that. Maybe make something up about needing to be there during the day, since Dr. Glen isn't there that often at night. Besides, I don't know how I am going to manage being there cleaning at night with just Jake and I if he shows up."

"Jake, is there a specific time you know Dr. Glen will be there?" Kate asked, as Jake was the only one in the group consistently at the clinic during the day.

Meg gave Jake a moment to process then offered the letter board. "REGIONAL CENTER CONING BACK TOMORROW. DR. GLEN NEEDS TO BE THERE."

Meg considered for a moment. "Huh. That just might work.

Do you know what time?" "10:00" Typed Jake.

"Ok. So now we have a time and place. What are wc going to set up?" Harvey asked and they sat for a minute, each considering.

"How about if I tell Meg that I need to work late Saturday?

Maybe I say something about Harvey going to a concert and so I figure I'll stay at the clinic late? We could do it under the premise that it's the end of the month and it's easier for me to finish up my paperwork if I'm there by myself." Noreen proposed.

"That sounds like a good plan to me, but I'm not comfortable with you being at the clinic by yourself, Noreen." A concerned look crossed his face.

"Oh. Right!" Noreen acknowledged. "What do we do about that?"

Adam started typing and Noreen paused. "WE CAN MAKE A DUMMY." Adam said.

"That's a great idea, Adam!" Kate cheered her son.

"Maybe we can make a dummy and put it in Noreen's chair with her back to the door. We'll turn some music on and have the lights on low. Then, when Glen overhears Meg's phone call she shares that she needs to return something to Noreen.

Noreen says she'll be at the office until about ten if she wants to drop it off. That allows for them to come after the sun sets. Not sure, but am thinking hit men like to be inconspicuous! Ha." Jerry received some eye rolls for his efforts at attempting light- heartedness.

"I have a vintage 'Annie' dummy we could use." Noreen shared.

"What are you doing with a vintage Annie dummy, Noreen?" Jerry asked, mocking a disparaging tone.

"Well, if you must know, way back when I was in college I taught CPR to help pay bills and it was just at the point where the new dummies were coming out, so someone donated it to us. I just never dealt with donating or selling it. I think I kept thinking it might come in handy for a Halloween decoration or something so it's just been sitting in its' box in the garage."

"And, I happen to have a wig that's almost the exact dusky blond of Noreen's hair." Kate added.

Raising his eyebrows a tad and gesturing at Kate's long brown hair, Harvey teased. "Why do you need a wig?"

"Halloween. I actually dressed up as Noreen at a typing get together last Halloween."

Adam, wearing a wry smile, had been working on a communication as they joked shared, "Did you hear about the dummy that robbed a bank?"

"Ha. No haven't heard about that. Tell me more!" Harvey took the bait.

"THE POLICE ARE QUESTIONING THE VENTRILOQUIST AS HE MAY HAVE HAD A HAND IN IT!" Adam shared the punch line and they all laughed.

Bringing the group back to their planning Harvey spoke next. "Ok. So tomorrow Meg will tell Noreen over the phone that she needs to return a letter board she had borrowed. Noreen will tell Meg, which Meg will repeat so Glen can hear that she will be at the clinic until around ten on Saturday night. Let's have her say she'll leave the back door open for Meg. That way, we will only have one door to monitor." Harvey paused. "And, of course, we'll make the dummy look as much like Noreen as possible and sit it in the chair with her back to the door. What do you guys think about letting the police know?"

"Well, I looked it up and in California you can record a conversation without consent if you reasonably believe it is necessary to protect your personal safety or the safety of others. Maybe we should have looked it up before we did it, but good to know that we are covered. Anyways, we can totally show it to the police because we were worried about Noreen's safety." Jerry said. "Given that, I say we meet with the police."

"I third that!" Noreen declared and they all agreed about calling the police.

They finished up with their plan and signed off their computers, designating Harvey and Noreen to call the police.

They sat and chatted out on the patio for a few minutes, then Harvey reached for the phone. "OK. We shall see what kind of response we get now!" He dialed.

Thankfully, it was a different officer than the one who had dismissed their concerns - this officer was attentive and concerned when Harvey told him their story. He was alarmed when they played the recording for him,

"This sounds very serious. I'm going to hop in the car and head right over," the officer stated.

Both Harvey and Noreen were relieved he was taking them seriously.

"Renews my faith in the system!" Harvey said with Noreen shaking her head in agreement. Harvey leaned over and pulled her into his arms. "I don't know what I would do without you!" he breathed into her hair. They sat there holding each other for what must have been about ten minutes until the doorbell rang.

They showed Officer Tom Chopper the emails and shared what Jake had overheard. Officer Chopper's voice was grave when he spoke. "Yeah. Not that you didn't already suspect this, but it definitely seems like he is trying to kill you, Noreen. But we will do everything we can to have that not happen!"

"On that note, our group ended up meeting today and came up with an idea I wanted to share with you." Harvey told him.

Officer Chopper was impressed with their plan, if a little wary at involving them in a sting. He agreed to let Harvey and

Jerry be at the stake out in case the police had any questions. He also recommended that Noreen stay at home with a police officer stationed outside. "Better safe than sorry." he said soberly.

Harvey and Noreen walked Officer Chopper to the front door.

As they passed through the family room Officer Chopper remarked on a gallery wall of family and friends over the years. "Is this your family?" He stopped.

"Yep. And friends." Noreen answered.

Officer Chopper stopped in front of a picture of Adam typing with Noreen at the Big Bear Lake house he grew up in, not far from the house he currently lived. "Is that Adam?" he asked.

"It is!" Noreen answered, surprised he knew Adam. Officer Chopper was looking at the photograph. His voice,

when he spoke, was a little incredulous. "So you are the one who helped him with his typing and communication?"

"That's her!" Harvey jumped in before Noreen could answer.

He was so proud of her work and the impact she had made. "My family has been friends with Jerry's original family. We were all devastated hearing the news that he had autism and might not be able to communicate well - ever. We were there before and after he started his typing. The difference it made in Adam and his families life was so huge. But, *MAN* have they taken some grief with all the hairy eyeballs and not so thinly disguised innuendos that they are somehow guiding my nephew's hand or giving him subtle cues that he picks up on now that he is independent. " Officer Chopper paused and stuck out his hand to Noreen. "It is truly an honor to meet you!"

Noreen reached forward, ignoring his hand, and gave him a big hug. "Well, I have to say that it has been an honor for me. There aren't many people who get to do something they love for a living. I do."

After seeing him out, Noreen and Harvey called the adults in their group, informing them of their interaction with Officer Chopper. Things were moving forward.

Expert Opinion

Reading Neurology, Prompt Dependency And Thigmotaxis

How Could An Autistic Person Pick Up On The Written Word Without Being Taught?

One question skeptics of the supported typing techniques have asked is, "How can people teach themselves how to read without formal instruction?" Many accounts of supported typing indicate that a person with autism has somehow picked up on the written word, and somehow was holding this inside until someone presented a letter board to them.

Clinical Observations And Autobiographical Accounts

First, I want to address opportunities with written words. Interestingly, many individuals with autism, including my son, (Filipek et al., 2013) have enjoyed watching Wheel of Fortune. My son also enjoyed watching Disney sing along videos where there was a bouncing ball on the words to a song, as well as the children's singer, Raffi. He first typed with his father showing him he knew the ABCs - something he could easily have picked up watching Wheel of Fortune. His first word with me was Raffi, a word he had seen hundreds of times watching a favorite children's video.

Other personal accounts from parents and typers regarding access to written words:

Earlier in the day while Sesame Street was on, I could see the letters and mathematical shapes better than the people and puppets who flickered among them. In the same way I gleaned a great deal of fragmented information from the news and current affairs each night, as well as quiz programmes favoured by Dad, because there were clear words shown on the screen which the announcer or presenter emphasised. (Biklen, 2005)

And,

For example, my father liked to watch the PBS Newshour every night, and he would always have the closed captioning turned on because English was not his native language, and it probably helped him learn more vocabulary. As a result, every week I would get at least five hours of text learning until I eventually could identify them on other things like the newspaper or in magazines which I loved flipping through. I can't say when I learned to read, but by the time I was going to Kindergarten I knew enough of my letters and numbers to find the constant worksheets we were being given rather frustrating because they were too easy in the lesson but too hard in what we had to do with them, like drawing a picture or coloring inside the lines. It seemed like all the focus was on the latter, and no one thought I could know the former. (Biklen, 2005)

So, there is evidence of opportunity to interact with the written words. Let's turn next to how the brain is connected in people with autism.

Imaging And Experimental Evidence

The ventral, or bottom, visual pathway processes pictures and objects, but has also been posited to process whole words and their meanings. (Cohen & Dehaene, 2004 Further, the ventral stream has been shown to be efficiently connected in persons with autism. (Kell et al., 2013. Therefore, it is conceivable that, especially given the statements above, that individuals with autism would be able to pick up on the written word when it is presented in meaningful ways. This aligns with research by Dawson and colleagues that examine block design performance on Raven's Progressive Matrices, which uses shapes and logic, and found that persons with autism performed significantly better on Raven's Progressive Matrices as compared to the Wechsler Intelligence Scale (Mottron et al., 2006. While Raven's Progressive Matrices require little motor ability or speech, the Wechsler Intelligence Scale has several items that require speech and motor ability.

Lastly, indicative of reading knowledge, using a whack-a-mole type game, a recent study looked at combinations of letters that were either randomly selected or from words and sentences, recently used. Investigators found that over half of the 31 participants with non-verbal autism demonstrated anticipation of the next letter in a sequence when the letters were part of a meaningful sequence. For example, if the letters were "tell", the participant would move to the e after the t quicker as compared to when random sequence of letters were presented, demonstrating that, similar to literate individuals, they anticipated the next letter (Jaswal et al., 2024.

Why Would The Studies Have Shown Such Strong Influence, As Well As A Lack Of Validated Communication From The Typer, If There Is Valid Communication With This Method?

The Neurology Of Influence, Prompt Dependency/ Thigmotaxis

Nicoli et al. 2023 proposed that touch may reduce the "cognitive load" with assisted typing, as is seen in individuals with motor difficulties due to stroke or Parkinson's disease.

Researchers have found that increasing cognitive load when doing balancing activities such as walking on a line puts extra "load" on balance when walking. Put simply, comparing a person's walking while not focusing on a cognitive task to a person's walking when they are focusing on a cognitive task, such as spelling a word backwards, they have less balance control. (Small et al., 2021 Nicoli and colleagues theorize that the touch provided in assisted typing lessens the postural control needed when typing, a cognitive task. They further go on to propose that even though touch may assist the motor system with cognitive tasks, that does not mean there is not a potential for influence, through the ideomotor effect.

Though the ideomotor effect is a reasonable hypothesis for why there was influence when typers were given touch or resistance, studies that looked at this phenomenon in autism found that this pathway may be impaired in autism. The ideomotor effect is the phenomenon of involuntary or unconscious movements triggered by ideas thoughts or expectations. For example when a typical person watches a person reach for a piece of food and eat it, their mouth musculature shows increased activation. This is not seen in persons with autism. Presumably if musculature is not activated associated with an idea such as eating, it would also be less likely that the ideomotor effect is responsible for the influence.

Cattaneo, L., Fabbri-Destro, M., Boria, S., Pieraccini, C., Monti, A., Cossu, G. et al. (2007). Impairment of actions chains in autism and its possible role in intention understanding. *Proceedings of the National Academy of Sciences*, *104*(45), 17825-17830.

Fabbri-Destro, M., Cattaneo, L., Boria, S., & Rizzolatti, G. (2009). Planning actions in autism. *Experimental brain research*, *192*(3), 521-525.

Further, I propose that the unique brain connectivity in autism further lends itself to influence. That is, the differential brain connectivity from the supplementary motor and premotor area (higher motor areas) and within the frontal (front part of the brain) cortex in general lends itself to an over reliance on external cues for movement, and difficulty with self-initiated movement. Function of the SMA and PMA include self initiated movements. If the PMA and SMA are not well connected to the primary motor area, it is plausible this lack of good connection would lead to difficulty with self-initiated movement.

Beyond self-initiated movements, there is a behavioral observation in animal research called thigmotaxis. One example of thigmotaxis is when an animal swims around the edges of a container rather than moving into the middle of the container to find a ledge to climb up on.

Animals with lesions in the frontal lobe, the area of the brain most affected in autism, do this. (Devan et al., 1999) Children with autism are 'thigmotaxic' in that they may tend to walk around the edge of a wall, or they may like to lay on the floor. When we did a pilot study examining gait differences in children with autism, we noted they tended to change the way they walked if there were lines on the floor, or the edge of a rug to walk on. The autistic participants would walk on the edge of the carpet or lift their feet up to miss lines we had put on the floor for measurement purposes. We did not see any typical participants do this. Conceivably, the prompt dependency and 'thigmotaxic' behavior seen in autism makes them unusually reliant on external sensory cues to support movement, and potentially more easily influenced by the same cues. To review, a major challenge with ABA therapies is prompt dependency. In a 2014 article Jones and Zarcone describe the issue:

> Prompt dependency is a common problem for children with intellectual and developmental disabilities and *especially* for children with autism spectrum disorder (ASD). Clark and Green (2004)

defined prompt dependency as an individual's correct responding being dependent on the controlling prompt of the therapist with little progress made in fading the prompt. This may occur as a result of the continual prompting that many children with ASD receive during one-on-one academic instruction, or may be related to processing deficits (Hume et al. 2009). Many children with ASD are taught specific skills using least-to-most (LTM) prompting (Horner & Keilitz, 1975). In LTM prompting, also known as a prompting hierarchy, learners are given a verbal instruction, followed by successively more intrusive prompts if they fail to respond accurately. The verbal prompt is followed by a model prompt in which learners are shown the correct answer and if they do not respond or respond incorrectly, they are physically guided to answer correctly.

So, autistic persons rely on external cues, or prompts, to be able to execute a learned skill and have difficulty breaking out of relying on that prompt, most likely due to differential brain connectivity. Other than brain connectivity differences, looking back on the autobiographical account by Chandima Rajapatirana may shed some light on a possible behavioral clue to thigmotaxic behavior. If a person has less body awareness if they are not moving or touching something, leaning against a wall or sinking into a couch would give greater body feedback.

[The] knack of knowing where my body is does not come easy for me. Interestingly I do not know if I am sitting or standing. I am not aware of my body unless it is touching something. Your hand on mine lets me know where my hand is. Jarring my legs by walking tells me I am alive.

I propose we also see this in the way a person with autism may grab his mom's hand to bring her to something he wants. He wants a juice box, but doesn't know how to open the refrigerator, or put the straw in the juice box, so he reaches for mom.

Aside from thigmotaxis, other possible confounding factors affecting influence include testing anxiety and accompanying emotional motor consequences; the experience of the facilitator as well as the FC user; the extended ability to practice a particular test; and processing time and/or difficulties with naming. While there is evidence from some studies of independent passing of information, there is substantial evidence that the facilitator can influence what is typed.

The studies that *do* evidence passing of information unknown to the facilitator appear to control for knowledge unknown to the facilitator by having the facilitator out of the room rather than using controls such as headphones or visual blocks, which can affect motor output and may enhance the ideomotor effect. In the many of the "blinded" studies that show influence, the facilitator was shown a picture or object, sometimes the same but sometimes different. In the studies that show message passing from the typer, the knowledge of what was going to be typed was handled by the person being out of the room. If you know what object is to be named/typed, you might subconsciously lean towards a particular letter. If you don't know what word is to be typed, you can't be influenced subtly. If you see a picture, you are more likely to unintentionally give cues towards letters.

Beyond thigmotaxis and being cued by a facilitator, there is evidence that both anxiety, visual changes and loss of hearing can impact motor control. (Carpenter & Campos, 2020; Greenwald, H. S., Knill, D. C., & Saunders, J. A., 2005). It is conceivable that the testing procedures that used headphones or visual blockers would affect motor control, amplifying the tendency of thigmotaxis and ideomotor effect. I suggest all of the above factors may come into play.

In summary: 1) Persons with autism can learn words because the ventral stream of their visual system is efficiently connected. There is evidence that this pathway processes not only pictures and objects, but also whole words and their meanings. 2) Frontal lobe brain connectivity is inefficiently connected and may impede control over voluntary movements. At the same time, the short U loop connections that process proprioceptive input as one is activating muscles are efficiently connected in persons with autism. Further, these connections provide an alternate avenue to access higher level motor areas in the frontal lobe as each U loop is connected to the next, thus facilitating control over voluntary movement. 3) Brain connectivity differences in individuals with autism make them particularly susceptible to influence.

Carpenter, M. G., & Campos, J. L. (2020). The effects of hearing loss on balance: a critical review. *Ear and hearing, 41*, 107S-119S.

Greenwald, H. S., Knill, D. C., & Saunders, J. A. (2005). Integrating visual cues for motor control: A matter of time. *Vision Research, 45*(15), 1975-1989.

Small, G. H., Brough, L. G., & Neptune, R. R. (2021). The influence of cognitive load on balance control during steady-state walking. *Journal of biomechanics, 122,* 110466.

Nicoli, G., Pavon, G., Grayson, A., & Emerson..., A. (2023). Touch may reduce cognitive load during assisted typing by individuals with developmental disabilities. *Frontiers in Integrative*

....

Devan, B. D., McDonald, R. J., & White, N. M. (1999. Effects of medial and lateral caudate-putamen lesions on place-and cue-guided behaviors in the water maze: relation to thigmotaxis. *Behavioural brain research.*

Testing The Theory Kris' Camp/Act Pilot Study

One possibility for testing the hypothesis of thigmotaxis and to describe the resistance used with facilitation support is to measure muscle activity of the typer and facilitator, using a protocol that assesses independent message passing as well as influence, while controlling for confounding factors that may affect or even enhance the possibility of influence. Many of the studies that have evaluated independent message passing have used protocols where the typer types a word to describe a picture or object, and many had distractor conditions where different pictures were presented to the typer and their communication partner. In one published study, where there *was* clear message passing, a story was read that the typer later answered questions about. (Weiss et al., 1996 In this study there was no condition where the facilitator saw something different than the typer, limiting influence. And, the facilitator was out of the room rather than having visual or auditory blocking, limiting any affects on motor output .

Weiss, M. J. S., Wagner, S. H., & Bauman, M. L. (1996). A validated case study of facilitated communication. *Mental retardation.*

This is important because whether thigmotaxis, the ideomotor effect or, most probably, both are responsible for the influence we see, if we are looking for independent message passing in a design it is important to control for confounding influence.

Alternatively, in order to study the influence, we need to incorporate a trial that tests for whether the influence we see in the studies that have been done is in fact ideomotor and thigmotaxic influence, or if the facilitator is indeed guiding the typer. That is, did the typer intend to type something different but was motorically influenced, but initially intended to type a different letter? Or, if the influence is simply the typer letting him or herself be guided by the facilitator.

In order to test the hypothesis, we need to investigate the muscle activity of the typer and facilitator. If the movement with FCT is backwards pressure, or even a simple touch to the arm or shoulder, this should look different than the EMG profile of guiding the movement in a hand over hand guiding way. In order to test the hypothesis for thigmotaxis, we would want to look at eye movements as well as EMG activity, explained more below.

A few years ago at a couple of programs where individuals with autism type, and where I worked, we tried a paradigm to evaluate this theory. Participants, including support staff and typers, wore Myo armbands. Myo armbands, developed to control computers virtually, can also be used to track EMG and spatial data. (Rawat et al., 2016)

We set up a simple 3 trial paradigm: 1) The typer and supporter were shown the same word. Instructions, written on a sheet of paper, were for the facilitator to help the person type the word. For the typer it was to type their word. 2) The typer and supporter were shown words that diverged. "There" and "their", for example. Instructions, written on a sheet of paper, were for the facilitator to make the person type the word. For the typer it was to type their word. And, 3) the typer was shown a word with the facilitator out of the room. The instruction was to type the word.

Extending this design, inspired by Weiss et al.1996, we read and wrote (multi modal presentation[2]) a short paragraph with the facilitator out of the room. Then we read out loud as we wrote three questions related to what was written and read. For example, the author wrote about going to the beach and then asked where the story took place.

Observations we made included: 1) In the influence trial two of six of the typers clearly looked at their letter (observer agreement) before easily going to the facilitator letter.

Alternatively, when neurotypical staff participated in this trial, we saw a "tug of war". 2) There was message passing, by three of eight participants, both with a single word as well as words that were meaningful to the story shared. For example, one participant typed "by water" when asked where the story took place (the beach). Moving forward, given that

---

[2] In the Klin article above there was a finding that toddlers with autism attended more to multimodal (visual and auditory at the same time) stimuli.

it appeared that participants may look at their letter first in the influence trial, it might be helpful to use an eye tracking device to measure this, similar to Grayson and colleagues 2012.

Grayson, A., Emerson, A., Howard-Jones, P., & O'Neil, L. (2012). Hidden communicative competence: Case study evidence using eye- tracking and video analysis. *Autism, 16*(1), 75-86.

Klin, A., Lin, D. J., Gorrindo, P., Ramsay, G., & Jones, W. (2009). Two-year-olds with autism orient to non-social contingencies rather than biological motion. *Nature, 459*(7244), 257-261.

Weiss, M. J. S., Wagner, S. H., & Bauman, M. L. (1996). A validated case study of facilitated communication. *Mental retardation.*

Rawat, S., Vats, S., & Kumar, P. (2016). Evaluating and exploring the MYO ARMBAND. 2016 International Conference....

Putting The Plan In Place

They had decided to meet at Noreen's and Harvey's. Even Kate, Jerry and Adam made the trip again from Big Bear.

Though Harvey, Noreen, Meg and Jake could have set up the cameras and dealt with Donovan, they all wanted to be together. Safety in numbers or something like that - at least it felt safer to be together, though Michelle and Nick had to beg out again as Nick was having difficulty with dysregulation.

A breeze flew from the west and the smell of jasmine floated in the air over Harvey and Noreen's back patio. It was a gorgeous sunny morning and the sun was just starting to burn through the morning fog. The temperature had climbed to the mid-seventies but the house threw shade over them. Between that and the breeze, the group appreciated Noreen putting throws out for each of them.

The group also appreciated Noreen's dedication over the years to making the perfect cinnamon roll. Ten minutes after Adam, Kate and Jerry had arrived, Noreen brought the rolls out from the oven along with some fresh squeezed orange juice and a big bowl of fresh blueberries..

Several minutes later found Meg, her stomach full of cinnamon roll, curled up under one of the throws on the couch, thinking about how the beauty of the day and the beauty of their friendship was overshadowed by the seriousness of what they were doing that day. The one word that seemed to be the running theme over the past few days sprang to mind as she thought about Donovan hating so much that he would stoop to hiring a hit man to kill off people who were helping kids to communicate - CRAZY!

She could tell Jake was a little on edge today, more periods of dysregulation. Mostly in that he seemed to need more of his comfort tools. Comfort tools like the Mardi Gras beads or the piece of a blanket that Meg had made for him when she was pregnant. Jake had carried that blanket around until the only thing left was a 4 by 4 square. Or, sometimes all Meg needed to do was to put Joni Mitchell on, or break out into song herself.

She'd recently started to use the deep pressure squeezes to music Noreen had shown her, which really seemed to help."

Meg imagined being able to communicate more countered the dysregulation too. She'd hate to think how Jake's regulation would be if he didn't have his newfound way to communicate.

Today though, she imagined Adam's presence was calming to him. She wondered if Jake had a sense of belonging with Adam. He felt seen - like when you meet up with an old friend who truly knows you. No need for explanations.

They went back and forth in a conversation around the cinnamon rolls. Adam had started with a reference to the new Coffee and Cinnamon Roll song that was flying around on TikTok. "COFFEE AND CINNAMON ROLLS. COFFEE AND CINNAMON ROLLS. GIVE ME THAT SPECIAL BLEND FROM SATURDAY TO SUNDAY."

Jake had laughed and typed. "WHAT DID THE CINNAMON ROLL SAY TO THE COFFEE?"

Adam searched for the answer for a good couple minutes. "I GIVE UP. WHAT DID HE SAY?"

Jake started giggling while he typed. "LET'S ROLL TOGETHER AND MAKE A GREAT PAIR!"

Jake got so giggly that Meg had to push back more on his arm, giving more resistance as they typed. It wasn't so much to steady his hand as it was to give more input to combat the added emotion. Noreen had given a brain pathway explanation, but she didn't remember it. She just knew that Jake calmed some and was able to type more when he was having more emotions and she gave more resistance.

"I see what you mean that when Jake is having more emotion - wether it be good emotions or not so good. It feels like when he is dysregulated at all, the resistance brings him back down to a calmer state." Meg turned to Jake excitedly, "Do you feel that way too Jake?"

At Meg and Jake's invitation, Noreen took over giving support and Jake typed. "I DO FEEL THAT. IT'S LIKE MY TURBULENT RIVER OF EMOTION MEETS SOME GENTLING BENDS IN THE RIVER PATH AND I CAN THINK."

"Great way to put it, Jake." Noreen giggled to herself. "My turbulent river of emotion, ha. Couldn't have put it better myself!"

After chatting a bit more and cleaning up the patio, the group headed over to Noreen's clinic. They had decided to take two cars. They weren't sure what Tony and Vito did before a job, and decided that Meg and Jake would go with

Noreen and Harvey in their car, while Jerry and Kate's rode in Jerry's truck.

While Noreen, Harvey, Jake and Meg would park in the front of the building, the others would follow a few minutes behind and pull in the back. There were overgrown shrubs in the back and so they thought that between the shrubs and how they would park the Suburban, it would be difficult to see what they were doing. Not great, they realized, in terms of if there was actually someone trying to hide out to break in, but good that it wouldn't be easy for the men to see what they were doing, if they were watching. Not a big deal. Lots of folks put up security cameras these days, but they would still prefer Tony and Vito didn't know they had just put security cameras up today.

As Noreen pulled into the clinic parking lot she got that feeling in her gut she had when she was driving down the mountain the day her brakes went out. She restrained herself from looking around the area for someone who might be watching them. Instead she glanced over at Meg and by the look on Meg's face, she wondered if Meg felt the same thing. Noreen smiled at Meg, if it came out a little wanly.

Tony and Vito sat at a window table at a cafe across the street from Noreen's clinic. They watched as Noreen, Meg and Jake pulled into the parking lot and sat for a few minutes talking.

They couldn't hear anything of course, but they could tell they were laughing.

"I wonder why this guy has it in for her?" Vito wondered out loud. "I mean she looks nice. She helps kids talk. Seems a little different than our usual targets."

"You're telling me. Almost comes across a little Mary Poppins- like."

"Yeah. It's nice to have the work, but I'm feeling a little funny about this one." Tony commented then took a bite of pancakes.

"Really?" asked Vito. He couldn't think of a time when Tony had expressed discomfort about a job.

"I said a little. Certainly not enough to stop me. Just was saying this one feels different." Tony shrugged his shoulders.

Noreen Meg and Jake positioned themselves in Noreen's office. While the others worked on setting up the cameras, they had planned on doing a typical session, partly on the off chance that they were being observed and partly to calm their own nerves.

Noreen started out alternating rhythmic deep pressure squeezes with heavy push ups over a therapy ball to activate Jake's muscles and facilitate his body awareness. The theory was that because the brain/body maps that told Jake where his body was were not well connected, he had a hard time knowing where his body was in space. At the same time, there were U-loops in Jake's brain that were activated every time Jake moved. These U-loops were over-connected in Jake's brain. So, aligning this neurology with autobiographical accounts like Noreen's friend who said that he didn't feel his legs unless he was stomping them, they did things that activated the U-loops so that Jake could feel his body better. The push ups over the ball were to give a lot of input to Jake's hands prior to typing.

Because they anticipated it would be stressful to be there knowing Donovan's hit men might be close by they had agreed to just work on set work - filling in blanks; multiple choice and even copy typing. Both Noreen and Meg had stressed to Jake that it had nothing to do with how smart he was, it was about how to best deal with the stress of the day, but if he had something he needed to tell them he could slip it in any time.

Beyond doing set work, Noreen shared that she wanted to try some new fun things. So after they finished their squeezes and push ups, Noreen brought out some paddle drums. Noreen loved working with music therapists, especially those that used rhythm to support movement, because they had such an intuitive sense for which supports they could use in the moment. Noreen was good at the rhythms of communication.

Neurodevelopmental music therapists were really good at the rhythm of movement.

For the next twenty minutes Noreen and Jake used the drums in a variety of ways with Jake smiling almost the entire time.

They walked forwards and backwards practicing starting and stopping while hitting the drum. They worked on eye movements, alternating swinging on the therapy swing with hitting targets on the drum. Noreen liked it because it really worked and she couldn't think of a client who didn't have a good time while doing it. Jake liked it because it was fun. Partly because of the interaction with Noreen, partly because it was fun to play the drum. But mostly, Jake loved it because with the rhythm he could move so much easier. When Noreen said stop he could stop! When she said go he could go!

While Jake, Meg and Noreen did their work inside, the others had pulled the Suburban close to the back wall above the door where they had planned on putting the camera. Jerry climbed on top of the Suburban as kind of a make shift ladder.

"Be careful up there Jerry!" Kate warned. Jerry was known for being less than graceful at times and had earned the nickname butterfingers at work. Last time he had hurt his back. It was just a month ago when he missed his chair when going to sit down at work. He was laid up for a week and Kate did not want a repeat. Jerry was many wonderful things but patient when he was ill was not one of them.

"What? Who are you kidding? I'm like Simone Biles up here.

I could do a back flip and land on my feet!" Jerry countered. "Simone Biles my eye!" Kate shook her head. "You just keep both feet on the roof."

But just as Kate said that, Jerry slipped. One foot went off the side of the truck and the other knee went down in an unnatural position. "OWWWW!!! Fuh...!" Jerry censored himself, and caught the roof rack just before he would have fallen.

"Jerry!" Kate and Harvey exclaimed, then everyone fell silent for a moment.

Jerry took a deep breath. "I'm ok. Not 100% sure about my knee, but I'm ok. " He paused. "I'm sorry Kate." He added, sheepishly, with deep felt sincerity. Jerry was prone to accidents, but had yet to learn the art of being careful.

They helped Jerry down and Harvey finished securing the camera. Then they headed straight to the local emergency department.

Tony and Vito watched the truck pull out of the clinic driveway. "Now that's my kind of getaway car!" Vito admired.

"Yeah. That works for me," Vito said as he watched Noreen, Meg and Jake exit the clinic.

Noreen Sets The Bait

It turned out that Jerry had a bad sprain, and the doctor prescribed a brace and a cane for at least the next six weeks. "She said I could be weight bearing as tolerated. How much weight do you think I can tolerate Harvey?" Jerry joked.

"I don't know. How about I climb up on your back and we give it a see?" Harvey teased back.

"Don't you dare you two!!" Kate admonished.

They had all spent the night at Noreen and Harvey's house. And, despite the circumstances, they all had a blast. For Jake, it was the first time he had had a friend over for the night. They ordered pizza and spent some time conversing after they had finished and the adults drank coffee. That was one of the hard parts of being reliant on support and typing to communicate. It didn't fit in with spontaneous communication over a meal. And, it was a lot of work for parents, usually mothers, to always be on top of things.

"YOU PLOWED THROUGH THAT PIZZA LIKE IT WAS YOUR LAST MEAL!" Jake teased Adam.

"OH AND YOU WERE JUST SAVING ALL THE ROOM FOR THAT AWESOME CHOCOLATE CAKE!" Adam teased back while giving praise to Noreen for her cake cooking. Chocolate raspberry cake was her second specialty.

Adam and Jake and the adults sat and chatted easily for a good hour. The conversation centered around supported typing - it's history; the controversy; and the neurologic basis

Noreen's friend had proposed. Then they turned back to ABA.

"Sometimes I feel like a jerk when I criticize ABA. I mean, there are some good things Skinner found. We all use ABA principles, we just don't think about it. When we're talking to someone and we look at them attentively while they speak to us, we are giving them positive reinforcement. Negative reinforcement is a little harder to understand, some say ignoring a behavior is negative reinforcement. But my understanding is it's removing something you don't like." Noreen paused in her comment. "However, I have repeatedly seen it play out over the years, with the principles being used adversely. The worst is the electric shock treatments that have been used, but the underlying lack of assuming competence is the big thing. Not looking harder or understanding better the underlying neurology. I can't tell you how many times ABA staff has said something negative about a child in front of them: 'Don't go near him—he'll kick you.' Or 'He doesn't talk.' Or 'He can't have that—he'll just throw it.'

"I know they don't use flinger flicks or other adversives much any more, at least not publicly, but I think the fact that punishment has been, and is still used in some circumstances, leaves somewhat of a residue that it's justified to treat someone poorly and call it treatment. Like with what you saw with your friend Billy, Jake. Billy can't control when he pulls people's hair. It doesn't support Billy by pulling his hair - supposedly showing Billy that it hurts. Of course Billy knows it hurts. He just doesn't have the brain connections that help him inhibit it. I really wish the field of applied behavior analysis would start learning about the neurology. In my opinion, teaching someone to not pull hair by pulling their hair doesn't work even if you have a typically connected brain. But if you have difficulties with praxis, you also have limited ability to control movements, especially with emotion. I just wish the field of applied behavior analysis would start teaching more about neurology. They say that you can only know the function of a behavior from what you observe. But if what you observe is a person not being able to sit for long, you can say it's because they don't want to do what you want them to do at that seat, or you could interpret it the way we do. If you're not feeling your body unless it is moving, then you are going to move unless you have an appropriate substitute. Analyzing behavior, especially for someone who had neurologic differences, solely on what you observe is too simplistic. There is a huge difference between a behavior being described as avoidance behavior (they get up from the seat - avoiding the task) and a behavior being described as accommodating sensory needs - his needs to feel his body."

Noreen took a deep breath. Everyone else had gone quiet. Not so much because they were surprised in any way by what Noreen was saying, more because they were interested in her viewpoint. "Ok. Sorry - I know I get long winded when it comes to these things."

Kate supported Adam to type. "I FOR ONE LOVE HEARING YOU TALK ABOUT IT, NOREEN. I SPENT TOO MUCH TIME LOCKED IN A CLOSET IN MY YOUNGER YEARS, SO I'VE CERTAINLY GOT A CHIP

ON MY SHOULDER, BUT I DO LOVE YOUR WELL REASONED OPINIONS."

Jake, with Noreen's support, picked up the thread. "WELL ADAM HAS BEEN ON THIS BLOCK MUCH LONGER THAN I HAVE BUT AM AGREED THAT ABA SEEMS CONDUCIVE TO THE LESS THAN KIND. ANY IDEAS ON HOW TO CHANGE THAT, NOREEN?"

"Afraid all we have at our disposal is to keep on keeping on with the truth. Science, at its best is objective, but when we involve people we also involve egos and I am afraid that there are many big eggheads in academia that have very fragile egos, which I think their owners are afraid will shatter if they accept a different idea than their own. Jerry was talking about it the other night.

"People often talk about how Copernicus put out a theory that the earth and other planets revolved around the sun. No one wanted to hear about it. Then, decades later Galileo was made to go through the inquisition and recant that same theory. It was hundreds of years before science and the general public accepted that the sun was the center of the universe. While that's probably one of the more famous stories, there are lots of others, including the refrigerator mother syndrome and autism story. It was probably 30-40 years until that theory was finally one for the history books. Heck, I'm not so sure there aren't some continued ramifications to this day." Noreen smiled at Adam and Jake.

"While I know there are several things we will learn about supported typing in years to come, on the whole, I believe in ten..." Noreen paused and thought for a moment. "Well, it might be more like twenty years at the rate we're going, but we will see a time where supported typing is understood for what it is - a therapeutic strategy based on clinical observations that supports people to more richly communicate. It will be accepted in the schools. It will be accepted by professional organizations."

Kate raised her glass of orange juice. "I will drink to that time!"

"Here here!" Jerry chimed in and they all raised their glasses in cheer.

Meg was nervous as she drove to the clinic later that morning with Jake in tow, They had gone over it a couple of times, but she really never fancied herself much of an actress. Actually, she was really shy in her teen years and had terrible stage fright. She guessed that was one of the good things about today. Her primary audience was one person. And she just needed him to hear part of the conversation. She just hope she didn't come off fake. Though as Noreen said, there was no reason to think Donovan had any idea that they knew.

"Ok Jake. Ready or not we're here!" Meg called out, a little anxiously, as they drove into the parking lot.

Jake vocalized in agreement. "Ahhh."

Meg noticed Glen meeting in the conference room with three women, whom she assumed were the regional center auditors. Meg wondered if he might be arrested for fraud and then realized that was the least of his worries if they were successful with their plan.

Meg and Jake put his things in his cubby and checked the board for who his assigned staff person was that day, Sheila. Neither Jake nor Meg cared for Sheila much. She seemed to have an arrogant way about her when Meg spoke to her. She had made a particularly disparaging remark about how Jake must be a real smart horse when Meg told her and another of her favorite staff, Teri, about Jake's typing. She told Meg that Jake must be a really smart horse, referring to the Clever Hans story. Clever Hans was a horse that could count by picking up on cues from his owner. Many of the detractors of supported typing claimed that this was all supported typing was. Meg wondered to herself how they rationalized someone who types and speaks their words. "That's a lot of cueing to pick up on for someone they claim is severely retarded, has autism, and thus doesn't pick up on social cues well. How could you cue someone like that on which of 26 letters to type?

Jake didn't like Sheila because she talked like a robot in an inauthentic sing songy syrupy voice. "Good job, Jake!" Jake knew it was meant to be encouragement, but instead it just made him feel dumb.

"It's ok." He thought. "It won't be long and I won't have to come here anymore." He knew his mom and Noreen had been talking about starting a small school out of Noreen's clinic. Plus, who knows what was going to happen at the clinic after Glen was arrested.

Sheila motioned to Jake and Meg from across the room. "Come on over guys and let's get started."

Meg gave Jake's hand a squeeze. "Ok little man. Here we go!", and they walked over to the table Sheila was standing at.

"So, I guess we're going over where Jake is on his goals and updating his program, right?" Sheila asked.

"Well, yes. I wanted to go over some recommendations his new speech therapist made and see if we could implement them here." Meg said. With everything that had been going on, she had no intention of having Jake stay at the clinic after this week, but this was the plan for their plan - her excuse to be at the clinic today.

Of course, in the back of her mind she still hoped she could change Sheila's mind, but there was really just a glimmer of hope there after everything she had been hearing from Noreen, Kate and Adam. Minds seemed to be made up on both sides but she was sure the truth lay on Noreen's side - as sure as Galileo must have been that the earth did indeed revolve around the sun.

Sheila hesitated for a minute, seeming to consider her words. "Sure." She hesitated again. "Though you know Jake can't read."

"How would you know?" Meg couldn't help asking, trying to keep the irritation out of her voice.

Sheila shrugged her shoulders and they all settled around the table. She caught Teri's attention from across the room and waved her over. "I guess you wanted Teri to be here too?"

"Yes. She did some of this with Jake and found it successful so thought it would be good if she joined us." Meg answered.

After Teri joined them, Meg brought out some letter-sized white boards. "Jake is doing some typing, but isn't accurate yet without support." Meg explained. "But, he is able to make choices on a white board and, well, you can use them in a variety of ways."

Meg went through the ways they had used white boards with Jake, keeping her eye on the door to the conference room. She hoped they would take a break soon. "One way we have tried using the white board is to use it as what Noreen calls 'the voice in Jake's head'. She says because he doesn't have efficient brain connections to help him control his voice, giving him a written external cue serves as the voice inside his head. The phrase Jake chose is "I can quiet my voice." Meg wrote it on the board and showed it to them.

Sheila suppressed an eye roll but Meg caught it. "Oh well, she thought. I tried."

"Another way to use it is to give Jake choices. It's a good way to start giving him some agency as Noreen says." She caught another stifled eye roll from Sheila but continued on. "So, for example, if you're starting some exercises, you could ask Jake which one he wants to do first. So in that way he gets some say."

Meg paused, glancing at the conference room where Donovan was. She could see the group standing.

"You can also use it to try and support his communication, if something is happening and you're unsure what he is trying to communicate, or you simply want to give him a choice on something. When you offer the choices, you always want to put a 'something else' or 'other' choice in case his answer isn't there. " Meg saw Glen come out of the conference room and head towards the break room.

"Sorry. I have to hit the restroom. I'll let Teri show you what they did. I'll be back in a minute." Meg excused herself and headed towards the break room.

Stopping halfway there, she surreptitiously pushed send on a text she had previously typed. It was a text to Noreen telling her it was time to call. She paused, pretending to look at a text on her phone. The phone rang and she walked into the break room. Glen was standing in front of the microwave waiting for it to finish.

"Hi Noreen!" Meg used a volume she thought Glen would hear over the sound of the microwave.

"Hi yourself!" Noreen said on the other end of the line, reciting the script they had prepared. She and Meg had agreed to make it as realistic as possible that they would keep to a script they had prepared.

"I wanted to drop off the device you lent Jake and I and was wondering when a good time would be." Meg said.

"I'll be working late at the clinic tonight if you want to stop by later. I should be there until about ten. " Noreen told her.

"You'll be at the clinic until ten?" Meg stated her line.

"Yes. I'll be there. Jerry will be picking me up around then.

My car is in the shop."

"Oh no! Your car is in the shop? Can't someone from work give you a ride?"

"No. Everyone leaves by five so I will be the only one there." Noreen read from the script in front of her.

"Won't you be scared being there all by yourself at night?" Meg noticed Glen standing near the microwave sipping his tea, seeming to glance at his phone but she was sure he was listening.

"Nah. The front door is locked. I'll leave the back door open for you so you can just come in."

"Are you sure you want to leave the back door open?" Meg asked, feeling a little chill up her spine. Never mind would it be scary for Noreen to leave the door unlocked. It was scary for her to be in the same building with Glen, much less the same room.

"Yes." said Noreen.

"Ok. Jake and I will stop by after his occupational therapy session, probably around seven."

"Sounds good. See you then!" Noreen signed off.

"See you then." Meg ended the call and turned to Glen. "Sorry. I didn't want to interrupt the sessions, so came in here."

"Sometimes I go outside if I want more privacy." Glen said. "I know." Thought Meg and turned to head back to Jake's session.

Glen's voice interrupted her exit. "Are you still doing that typing stuff?" Glen's tone sounded concerned instead of the disparaging tone she expected.

"Yes." Meg confirmed simply, not wanting to get into a discussion with Glen.

"It really is bad business." He really did seem concerned to Meg, which threw her off a bit.

How could he be concerned about Jake and her but at the same time be planning on killing Noreen? she thought. I guess us humans are complicated beings.

"I know you have misgivings about it, but you might want to look into it more - meet some of the folks who have done so well with it." Meg said and quickly left the break room so she missed Glen's eye roll and head shake.

Meg stayed for another hour. It was hard to watch Sheila work with Jake. It just felt so repetitive and disrespectful, especially now that she understood just how smart Jake was.

After Noreen finished her phone call with Meg, she called home. Kate and Jerry were there working on the dummy they would use for tonight. Kate had brought down a wig and they had dressed it up in one of Noreen's old dresses she didn't care about.

"Ok. We set the bait. Meg will call later and let me know how it went on her end. How are you guys doing?" Noreen asked.

Kate had answered. "Good! The dummy actually kind of looks like you from the back!" They both laughed. "We'll be over in about an hour."

They had decided to use an old suitcase of Harvey's to transport the dummy, just in case someone was watching. When they arrived at the clinic the parking lot in front was full so they went around back and Noreen let them in.

"Hey guys! I can't wait to see what it looks like!" Noreen welcomed Jerry and Kate in. Kate was carrying the suitcase as Jerry was using a crutch to keep the weight off his knee.

They set the dummy up in one of Noreen's desk chairs, her back to the observation window. They figured if the hit men came in and saw the back of Noreen's head, it would be easy to just take the shot through the window. That is, if they used a gun.

When talking through their plan, they got into a discussion of how they thought the most likely way Tony and Vito would try to kill Noreen was a gun. But then Jerry brought up that maybe they would use a knife? Strangle her? For a few moments it started to feel pretty morbid and scary to them all.

Then Adam joked, "MAYBE THEY'LL DO IT WITH A SONG!

KILLING ME SOFTLY WITH HIS SONG." And they all laughed. It didn't take away all the morbidness, but they all felt a bit better.

The good news was that no matter which killing method they thought of, there was no scenario they could think of where Tony and Vito would be successful, and no way they would be free men tomorrow if they showed up at Noreen's clinic tonight.

Noreen, gazing at the back of the dummy, asked. "Do you really think it looks like me from the back? Do you think this is going to fool them?"

Jerry stood next to where Noreen was, examining the dummy. "I actually do, especially if they're expecting Noreen to be there, not a dummy. There's a whole field of study looking into how our expectations can actually suppress sensory information coming in."

"Interesting. Does that mean that when I come home if I expect to see clean dishes, I will see clean dishes?" Kate teased Jerry.

"Well, I think your nervous system can only suppress minor changes." Jerry answered sheepishly. "I think coming home to clean dishes might just make you faint, so I'm actually looking out for you! "

"Maybe we need to get you some supports in place, Jerry! I think we tend to forget that about folks who are more integrated, but still have autism - those level 1 autism folks. I think sometimes it's almost harder for you guys, because people expect you to easily do tasks like clean the dishes. No one expects Jake or Adam to be able to wash dishes on their own, but when it seems easier for you, they forget you still have organizational challenges."

At Noreen's prompting Jerry had gotten an autism evaluation and concurrent diagnosis just last year. It shed a lot of light on challenges Jerry had had over the years - like having a hard time breaking his focus on something he was interested in - solving a computer issue, so that he could get something done he didn't want to do, like the dishes was one example. It gave both Kate and Jerry new insights into their marriage so that they were able to joke about things that used to have a whole undercurrent of resentment. But, they hadn't found a clear path for what to do about it. Having the diagnosis gave them an explanation, but they hadn't found a good therapist to work with. They would try for awhile, then back away when they didn't find resources.

Noreen made some suggestions, but she mostly saw level two and three autism clients so didn't feel she had particular expertise.

"Yeah. We'll follow up on some of those leads you gave us." Jerry said, referring to a couple recommendations Noreen had found for them.

Later that afternoon Meg, Noreen, Adam, Jake and Kate were at the house after Jerry and Harvey went to the clinic to prepare the stake out for tonight. They had been so absorbed with everything, neither Jake nor Adam had had the opportunity to say much. Both of them jumped at the chance when Noreen asked if they wanted to do a lesson and chat a bit.

Seated around the patio table, Noreen gave Jake and Adam the choice to read from the Giving Tree or to read a passage a scientist friend of Noreen's wrote on the neuroanatomy of autism and why it made supported typing made sense. Of course, the neuro passage was a little drier, but Noreen had found over the years that her clients hung on every word when she explained how she thought their brains were different - not better or worse, and why they acted in certain ways.

Jake and Adam both chose to read both. Noreen started off with deep pressure squeezes, alternating between Meg and Kate to assure they were giving enough pressure. She had found over the years that, probably due to being anxious about doing it right, parents tended to be very light on the pressure and Noreen found this was dysregulating for the kids. But the rhythmic deep input was calming. So Noreen took every chance to support parents using really deep pressure.

When Noreen had very first started doing squeezes, Jake was resistant and it made him anxious. But it only took a couple sessions of squeezes - the really deep kind, before Jake realized he didn't feel the need to move as he usually did and was more relaxed. He wasn't sure yet if he was more aware if his body, as Noreen had explained, but he did know it felt good.

Noreen picked up the paper she had printed out with her friend's theory and started reading.

"To understand a rationale for supported typing we need to consider what we now know about how the brain is connected differently in persons with autism. One particular question I want to address is how could someone learn to read without being formally taught? One possible reason is that the part of their visual system that processes pictures, objects but also whole words and their meanings is efficiently connected. From a clinical perspective, we see this in many of our clients being particularly good at doing puzzles, or remembering things visually like Stephen Wiltshire who flew over New York once and then was able to draw the skyline from memory. At least part of the visual pathways in the brain are working very well in persons with autism.

"At the same time, there has been a lot of research looking at how people with autism are able to understand and perform gestures - movements that have meaning attached to them. This can get very confusing because different fields call it something different, and even define it differently. Physical and occupational therapists most often call it apraxia and define praxis as the ability to think about how to do something, how to sequence a movement. A behavioral neurologist might use the term developmental dyspraxia instead of apraxia and define it as a disorder of producing meaningful gestures. An occupational therapist might use the sensory integration and praxis test to measure praxis. This test uses meaningless simple movements. On the other hand, a neurologist studying praxis would ask someone to pantomime a series of gestures. Show me how you would cut a piece of paper, for example.

"While the definitions are similar, I believe it is important because if we aren't talking about the same thing, we can misunderstand. An OT says a client has difficulties with praxis because she used a test that measures imitation of meaningless movements. A doctor, testing the ability to produce meaningful gestures, would also say that a person had difficulty with praxis if they didn't do well. Both are saying it is a disorder of praxis.

Yet they are measuring two different things.

"I don't think it affects how we do therapy - most therapists who understand the cognitive motor difficulties approach it generally that the person is capable, but is stuck in a body that doesn't do what they want it to. But, when it comes to understanding more about what is happening, it is important.

The skill of imitating a meaningless movement is a different brain pathway than the brain pathway responsible for producing and understanding meaningful gestures. We are using two different tests to measure praxis that measure two different brain pathways. Yet, we call it the same thing.

Finished reading, Noreen placed the paper on the table and gave the boys a few moments to process then asked. "What do you guys think? Does that sound right to you?"

Jake typed. "I FEEL MY BRAIN IS LIKE A POLAROID CAMERA SOMETIMES. I LOOK AT SOMETHING AND HAVE A PICTURE IN MY HEAD."

"I FEEL LIKE IMAGES OF PLACES I'VE BEEN OR EVEN WORDS FLOAT AROUND IN MY HEAD." Adam commented.

"Sometimes I wonder what it would be like to be able to switch bodies with one of you. I mean, when I hear you say things like you have words floating around in your head, I want to be able to experience what you do." Noreen looked from Jake to Adam. "It might surprise you that I, and probably most people, don't walk around with images or words floating around in our head.'

"REALLY?" Jake asked.

"Really." Noreen answered while she looked over at Meg who was looking confused.

"What I don't understand is what exactly is going on in Jake's motor system. Noreen, you had said it was easiest to think of as difficulty initiating inhibiting or sustaining movement. But then there's all this talk about praxis. It just gets confusing." Meg said.

"I like to think about it that from a pragmatic standpoint it is easiest to think of as difficulty with cognitive control over movement. So, when Jake is upset he has less brain capacity to stop himself from making loud noises. Or, if he is typing he needs cues to be able to keep going. 'Keep going, You can do it!' They're words of encouragement but you can also think of it as a prompt to keep going." Noreen explained. "The praxis stuff gets confusing. Mostly because even the experts are somewhat confused. Who knows maybe twenty years from now we will have a whole new name for it, specific to autism. But, for now you can think of it as part of the cognitive motor system. If you have dyspraxia, you have a hard time translating a thought into a movement. I wouldn't worry about it too much. I would just keep doing what your doing. You're very intuitive about how and when to give Jake supports."

Meg smiled. "Well, thanks for the compliment, but I think I've got a long way to go."

Noreen smiled back. "I have a music therapist who has a song she sings to the kids. It gets easier if you push through.

Sometimes I think we need to sing it to the parents too." And, they all laughed.

They chatted a bit more about brain pathways then Noreen read from The Giving Tree. An age old message about how what any of us truly needs is love. Adam had read it before, but this was Jake's first time hearing it.

"I LOVE THAT THE TREE GAVE SO LOVINGLY. BUT IT ALSO MADE ME SAD. I FELT THE BOY COULD HAVE BEEN A LITTLE MORE LOVING ALONG THE WAY."

"I felt that too, Jake. But I think it's the story that happens to so much of us along the way. We have more time to laugh and play when we're young and then seem to get caught up in being busy with life, only to find what we really want is love, companionship and comfort in our old age."

In form, Adam typed. "WHEN YOU COMING HOME, DAD? I DON'T KNOW WHEN, BUT WE'LL GET TOGETHER THEN. YOU KNOW WE'LL HAVE A GOOD TIME THEN."

"Lots of songs have incorporated that theme, but let's never get too busy for these friendships!" Kate gestured towards the group.

"I'll definitely drink to that!" Meg agreed and raised her ice water glass then glanced at her watch. "I think it's almost time for me to head over to the clinic."

They had debated whether to have Meg and Jake go to the clinic for real under the premise that she was returning the communication device. The group decided that it would be safe for Meg as it would still be light and the police, Harvey and Jerry had already set up shop with the police in a business that looked out onto the back parking area. Plus, they didn't want to give Tony and Vito any reason to not follow through if they were waiting for Jake and Meg to leave or to think something wasn't right. It was likely they were watching as Donovan probably would have shared with them that Meg was dropping by.

"Do you need anything? You have the device?" asked Kate. "Yep." replied Meg, a little anxiously. "Just a little nervous." "Ahhh." Jake vocalized.

"Just remember the police and Harvey and Jerry are listening in and watching. You'll be fine." Noreen reassured both Jake and Meg.

"It's ok, Jake. We'll be fine." Meg, gathering up her sweater, reassured Jake too, putting on a brave front for him.

Meg took lots of deep breaths as she drove to the clinic, only a five minute drive from Noreen's house. As she pulled into the parking lot she didn't notice a black Honda Accord parked catty- corner to the clinic parking lot. Tony and Vito looked out through the tinted windows at Meg's rear profile - all they could see as she drove past them.

"That must be the woman Donovan was referring to." Tony commented.

"I don't know." Vito responded. "It kind of looks like Noreen. Could that be her?"

"Huh." Tony said, hesitating. "Maybe?"

They saw Meg pull her car behind the clinic and disappear from sight and sat thinking for a couple moments.

"Should we follow her? I'm a little worried that that might be Noreen." Tony suggested.

"Yeah. We don't want to miss her - that's for sure. Maybe they're plans changed. Let's pull in back and then we can see her when she comes out."

Tony pushed the ignition button and pulled into the street and took a quick turn into the clinic parking lot. As they pulled in back they saw Meg's blue civic. They could see her silhouette. She was still sitting in her car.

Looking in the rear view mirror, Meg's heart froze as she saw the accord pull in behind her. She could see two figures. What should she do? She wasn't planning on going into the clinic, but she hadn't planned on seeing anyone, much less who she thought might be Tony and Vito.

Attempting to keep the plan in place, Meg took another deep breath and opened the car door, bracing a little for any impact. Would they shoot her? She honestly didn't know, but was relying on the fact that the police were watching and they had their own guns.

From their viewpoint, the police saw Tony and Vito drive behind the clinic. Just yards away from where Meg sat in her car.

"What the heck?" Harvey cried out in concern for Meg. Detective Mozzie, looking through binoculars for a moment, maintained a calm voice. "Remember, John and Tom are down there. They will make sure Meg stays safe.", referring to the two officers hidden in the shrubs.

"I sure hope so." Jerry, sitting with his knee elevated said. "I hope so."

They all held their breath. It seemed like time stopped in that moment as they waited to see what happened next.

Tony and Vito, holding their breath a little too, watched as the car door opened. Tony took his gun out of the glove compartment, placing it on his thigh as he waited.

Meg stepped out of the car, hearing her heart beating loudly in her chest. She glanced over at the Accord attempting nonchalance. It was funny how she debated tiny things in this moment. Should she look at the car or not look at the car? In any other situation, if there was only one other car in the parking lot, she figured she would probably attend to it even if only for a moment.

As she glanced their way, Tony and Vito realized this was a much younger woman than the picture they had seen of Noreen. Besides, she looked nothing like Noreen.

Tony rolled his window down and Meg froze.

"Hey! Took a wrong turn! Needed to stop to look at directions!" Tony called out to her and put the car in drive.

Meg let out a deep pent up sigh, got Jake out of the car and they walked into the clinic. Ten minutes later Vito and Tony watched them pull out of the parking lot.

They sat peering out a window partially obscured by bushes separating the back parking lot from the next building. One of the officers had brought a big jug of coffee and they all sipped on a cup.

Wanting to stay quiet they texted each other to while away the time, both Jerry and Harvey reflecting on how it was mildly frustrating *but* they didn't need any support and could type quickly.

"The cubs are close to missing the playoffs." Tom typed in response to Jerry's comment that this was going to be the year for his team. Jerry was born and raised in Chicago and, like so many from that area, was an avid fan.

"We didn't do so bad a week ago! Gave you guys a head start on warming up on a rematch!" Jerry typed back, referring to an exciting game the prior week where the Cubs won.

"I don't know about you guys, but this being confined to texting is giving me a new appreciation for how my son communicates. He has to have support to type on a keyboard." Jerry continued.

"Your son types to communicate?" Texted Bill, the other officer waiting with them. "My nephew has autism and does the same thing. It's been life-changing for him and he just started at Whittier College."

"That's what Noreen does. Well, one of the things she does, but maybe the most important." Harvey texted in.

Tom and Bill looked at Jerry and Harvey, a confused, angry look on their faces. "And someone is trying to kill her?"

Jerry and Harvey, almost simultaneously, shrugged their shoulders and raised their hands as if to say "Yeah. Go figure."

Tom and Bill inclined their heads in agreement and they all sat in silence for a few moments as they each contemplated why any one would want to kill someone like Noreen.

The sound of an engine pulling into Noreen's parking lot brought them all to attention, and they watched Tony and Vito's Honda pull in. They could see that each man pulled a gun from their belt as they moved toward the back door.

Tony and Vito took their job seriously. More out of a need for self-preservation than any sense of responsibility. They knew that if they messed up they might end up in jail, or dead. In their unique uneducated hit-man kind of way, they had worked out a system where they stopped about a hundred feet from their destination when arriving at a target so they could touch base on anything last minute they needed to say. From then on they communicated with hand gestures - things like imitating pulling the trigger on a gun and pointing to a person.

As they arrived at the back door to the clinic, Tony motioned to Vito to go first. Vito opened the door slowly, glancing in to make sure they weren't going to run into anyone. The hallway was dimly lit and they walked into the clinic.

They could hear soft music coming from the office and they followed the sound back to Noreen's office. They stopped as they got closer. Vito gestured for Tony to peer around the corner to check out the scene, pointing to his eyes then the observation window outside Noreen's office comically gesturing peeking around the corner.

Looking through the window, Tony could see the back of Noreen's head and gave the thumbs up or thumbs down gesture followed by a pulling the trigger. Vito peered through the window and gave two thumbs up and they both aimed their guns at the back of Noreen's head. A soft whistling sound marked the discharge from their silenced guns.

Needing to make sure they had finished the job, they entered the office. At first they were confused by the confetti they found on the floor, but when they approached the body it began to dawn on them something wasn't quite right. The makeshift book that Jake and Adam had suggested lay in front of the dummy.

Vito read out loud, his voice slowing as the words dawned on him. "Hit Men for Dummies..."

"I think we may have been set up. We got to get out of here!" Tony said, a tad densely and turned back towards the door.

"Not so fast." Tom advised, standing just outside the door. Bill stood behind the darkened observation window, his gun trained on the men in Noreen's office. "My partner has his gun pointed at you. Very slowly, put your guns down."

Tony started to put his gun down just as Vito made a run down the hallway, knocking over Officer Chopper. He flew open the back door and raced threw it, only to stumble over Jerry's outstretched crutch and fell flat on his face. Officer Chopper, hot on his trail, quickly restrained and handcuffed him. Officer Mozzie followed seconds later with Tony, handcuffed, in tow.

"An easy job, huh?" Tony complained to Vito.

A Big Sigh Of Relief

The group was eagerly awaiting her return when Meg arrived back at Noreen's house.

"Are you ok?" Noreen greeted her at the door with a big hug. "Whew!" Meg replied, putting her hand to her chest.. " I am pretty sure they drove into the parking lot after me, but they turned around."

"Oh my god!" Kate exclaimed. "You must have freaked out!" "Pretty much." replied Kate. "I think my heart literally

stopped for a minute there, but then they just called out to me that they had taken a wrong turn. I don't think I have ever been more relieved than when I made it back to Noreen's house."

Kate poured Meg a glass of wine and they say at the table out back with Jake and Adam. Adam typed a part of the Spider Bite song..

I WAS GLAD IT DIDN'T DESTROY YOU HOW SAD THAT WOULD BE 'CAUSE IF IT DESTROYED YOU IT WOULD DESTROY ME

"Thanks Adam." Meg laughed.

They sat for awhile, listening to Joni Mitchell, sporadically conversing, all waiting and wondering what was happening at the clinic. They watched the sun set and waited. Finally, an hour later both Noreen and Kate's phone rang. It was their perspective husbands letting them know Tony and Vito had been arrested and the police had them in custody.

Glen had opened a single barrel whiskey he had been saving for a special occasion. He sat in an armchair in his home office, jazz playing in the background. He had a deep feeling of satisfaction, anticipating a confirming message from Tony and Vito telling him the job had been done. He had slipped too far over the edge to have any feelings of misgivings or regret.

Glen looked over at the vivarium where his California King snake lived and he smiled. "Pretty soon there will be no energy left in the stupid typing crowd." He thought.

Expecting a vibration buzz on the phone Tony and Vito had given him, he was taken aback at the sound of the doorbell. He set his glass on the side table and headed to the door. Officers Chopper and Mozzie waited on the other side of that door.

Peering through the peephole, Glen saw two uniformed officers. He froze. Did they know? He took a deep breath and opened the door.

"Good evening, officers. What can I do for you?" Glen attempted a calm, cheery voice as best he could.

"Glen Donovan?" Officer Chopper asked. "Yes? What's this about?' Glen replied.

"You are under arrest for the attempted murder of Noreen Schack. Put your hand behind your back." Officer Mozzie moved behind Glen and placed the handcuffs around his wrist. Glen, in a stunned state of disbelief, could do nothing but comply.

Not To Be Silenced

Almost a year later found the gang of eight having breakfast at a diner close to the federal courthouse. It had certainly been a year as they followed the trial. Tony and Vito had been convicted of attempted murder as well as Glen. Though Tony and Vito refused to testify, the court had the recordings and emails. The court also allowed Jake's account of what he had heard as he had worked hard to be as independent as possible.

Jake was now able to do two handed typing with a support person standing behind and touching him on his shoulders - a skill he, his mom and Noreen had worked on relentlessly, and he had begun being able to speak his words, if a bit stilted. It was a little dicey at first, as the judge wanted to do a message passing test and Jake couldn't do it at first. He found he tended to freeze up and he either was unable to type any meaningful words, or he let himself rely on subtle cues from his mom in instances where he was supposed to type a specific word. They would start off with the first two letters correct and then his mom would shift slightly, anticipating the next letter, and he would go in that direction.

So, they spent most evenings and weekends practicing for a good couple of months, and Jake was easily able to pass a message at the end. On the day of his testimony, he had been nervous and had difficulty controlling his 'automatic' sounds. It started off and Jake couldn't stay seated. He would sit down and start typing a couple of letters, but then couldn't suppress the need to move, so he would stand up and jump in place, waving his arms as Meg and Noreen tried some regulation strategies. Luckily, the judge had a son with non verbal autism and was understanding of the difficulties Jake was having. He was also intrigued and hopeful about the typing, if a bit skeptical.

They took a recess and Jake, alternating with support from Noreen and Meg, climbed a flight of stairs twenty times, did some supported deep breathing and put some lavender essential oil lotion on his hand. It settled his nerves enough that he was able to return to the courtroom and finish his testimony. It only took the jury thirty minutes to come back with a guilty verdict.

Glen, watching the entire thing play out, had a hard time wrapping his mind around it. If he had a conscience, he would have felt extreme regret, but he did not. Instead he kept puzzling over how Noreen and Meg were 'controlling' Jake's responses. How could they have known what he said on the playground? How did they know where to look for his doctored books? He was far too narcissistic to even consider he had been wrong.

The group had wondered if he would say anything, maybe apologize, at the sentencing hearing today. Whether he did or did not, Jake, Adam and Noreen all had decided they wanted to make a statement.

Noreen's statement centered around her feelings, her fear, of being the target of hit men. She touched on the typing stuff when she closed saying, "The thought that if I was not here anymore would in any way influence the supported typing movement is crazy. It is real and it is here to stay, whether I'm here or not.

Adam's statement centered around the theme of how Noreen had blown doors open for him. Adam's statement was particularly impactful as he could read his words very clearly and only needed for the tablet to be positioned correctly by his mom before he could type, resting his arm on the table gave him enough proprioceptive support to be able to type his words.

Nick decided not to contribute as he thought Jake's statement said it clearly. "YOU THOUGHT YOU COULD SILENCE US, BUT YOU WERE WRONG!"

Expert Opinion

A Pilot Study And Some Notes On The Research

More On Why Doesn't The Typing Community Do The Validation Studies? Spoiler Alert: They Have.

We have previously discussed study design, and what scientists call "confounding factors" - in this instance factors that *contribute* to influence. While it is important to demonstrate authorship, in order to fully understand what is happening we also need to control for influence. In a recent correspondence with Katharine Beals, I sent her a copy of the scientific paper I wrote with much of the recent research that evidences praxis and motor learning differences. Her reply references the influence studies on her "anti"-supported typing website, www.facilitatedcommunication.org:

> ... we've looked at everything there is on (purported) apraxia and motor disorders in autism. If you want to convince people of the legitimacy of FC, there are two key things you can do. One is to participate in a rigorous, videotaped message-passing experiment conducted by an independent researcher.

> The other is to explain why the current account of autism as a socio-cognitive disorder that undermines language (and literacy)

acquisition is wrong and to provide an alternative account of autism spectrum disorders that does a better job accounting for all the data on autism, across the autism spectrum, and that makes better scientific predictions, across the autism spectrum. (A tall order, I recognize, given that the socio- cognitive take on autism has been accumulating massive amounts of corroborating research for about 8 decades).

It is important to remember that I had sent two papers detailing motor differences in autism - certainly not an exhaustive list - I arbitrarily picked a couple that showed motor differences and dyspraxia. Katharine Beals remarks on the website that she had not read these, so did. Yet, in her email she says "...we've looked at *everything* there is on (purported) apraxia and motor disorders in autism." So, obviously she is not familiar with *everything* there is on apraxia and motor disorders in autism, if she, by chance, hadn't read the two motor papers I picked relatively randomly.. Further, since I picked those two papers to demonstrate the research on movement difficulties, I would guess these aren't the only papers she hasn't read.

If you are wondering at the choice of a website, in a video on YouTube she expresses their (website contributors) delight at being able to get that particular website name (facilitatedcommunication.org), presumably in the hope people looking for information will be guided to their negatively biased website.

I reference this interchange between Beals and me because:

1) It highlights the lack of awareness about new praxis and motor learning research among, at least some, critics of supported typing; and 2) It emphasizes the importance detractors put on conducting studies that demonstrate the significant impact of influence. In other words, it sounds like the only research acceptable to folks who are heavily grounded on the detractor side is if someone were to videotape a successful message passing experiment, similar to the ones already done that showed influence, conducted by an "independent researcher", which shows how little trust there is on either side. Though I am not exactly sure what Beals was referring to when she put in the guideline of having an *independent researcher,* but I assume that she means it would have to be someone unassociated with typing in any way. So, even if I were funded to do the study mentioned earlier, and have it accepted in a peer- reviewed journal, she wouldn't trust it, similar to the research that is already out there.

From personal experience and personal correspondence, I understand that those involved in the initial FCT supported typing, there was a push to understand how to get people to be independent, which they did. I don't think anyone understood, or even had a strong theory, why there was so much influence in those early studies. So, the thought was to work towards independence. But, the critics suggested that even those who were typing independently, but still needed some support in terms of setting up the keyboard or having a familiar person close by were being influenced by subtle cues.

For example, they did much better if a parent was standing at the back of the room.

Critics have suggested that somehow independent typers are picking up on subtle cues to know which of 26 letters to select. (Howitt, 2023 , and Mostert 2012, e.g.)

As I worked with more and more people under this paradigm, and saw successes, I became determined to learn as much as I could about the autism brain and motor differences in the hopes of one day doing research. I thought the best way to tackle research was to understand the underlying neurology that would align with the findings in supported typing - what is the underlying neurology behind the influence? How was it possible these guys picked up on the written word without being formally taught? I wanted the answers to these questions.

My thought was that if we could understand the neurology, we could design experiments, as well as refine approaches, better. Obviously there is the potential for influence, but how do we test for the communication and motor differences without creating a design where we only see the influence. I summarize this in *The neurology of typing communication in autism. A summary*, Appendix 1.

Wait. At Least Some Of The Research Has Been Done?

From my interaction with Katharine Beals, it appears that some critics won't be satisfied unless typing advocates can figure out a way to redo the studies that showed the influence, but somehow demonstrate authorship. Because, there are studies demonstrating message passing by the typer - including one where someone was able to pass the original "influence" study; qualitative research including people who are now independent; as well as those who learned to speak their own typed words.

More recently, as mentioned, there have been studies showing people look at a letter before going to it, indicating that the typer had the intention of going to that letter. We found this similarly in the pilot study we did at Kris' Camp. Yet, when emailing with Katharine Beals she didn't address the above studies but instead suggested if I wanted to convince people of the efficacy of supported typing I needed to set up an "influence" study design and demonstrate authorship. Similarly, discussed further below, other researchers have discounted much of this research claiming somehow the person is being cued.

Grayson, A., Emerson, A., Howard-Jones, P., & O'Neil, L. (2012). Hidden communicative competence: Case study evidence using eye-tracking and video analysis. *Autism, 16*(1), 75-86.

Though there are some studies evidencing independent message passing with typing, importantly, beyond studies specifically looking at typing, there have been several studies looking at how praxis presents in autism. Further, there are studies looking at different motor learning profiles in autism, discussed above, which support observations made by typers and their advocates. Before closing the excerpt, let's look deeper at three studies that evidence authorship using touch support.

In chapter 7 of Biklen's, *Contested Words. Contested Science.*, a 1997 book describing, qualitatively, what we see in supported typing, Michael Weiss and Sheldon Wagner detail two case studies - one published in a peer-reviewed journal, where the typer demonstrated clear communication with facilitation. The authors of this chapter are two psychologists and start the chapter with "Finding ourselves writing this chapter for this volume on facilitated communication is somewhat remarkable." and cite a newspaper article where they were quoted *before* conducting the study:

Michael Weiss, a clinical psychologist who has worked with developmentally disabled children in New Bedford, is also concerned. "there's a rich tradition in how we judge whether something is true It gets reviewed by peers and has to pass a certain standard." he said. "What I'm unnerved about with the facilitated communication people is that there's a refusal to adhere to this standard." Asked why he thinks Dr. Biklen and company won't do such studies, Dr. Weiss replied, "What rings true in my ears is that the thing is a bloody hoax." (Sunday Standard-Times, New Bedford, Massachusetts, February 16, 1992.)

But the families and teachers Weiss and Wagner worked with pushed as they thought it was a valid technique.

And:

After lengthy discussions with families and teachers about the "Clever Hans" effect and experimenter bias, we finally arrived at some agreement in how we would begin evaluating the validity of this method with their children.

Following a detailed report on how they validated two typers communications, these authors close with:

> We entered this area of inquiry as hostile skeptics, looking to protect our clients from what we perceived is extremely dangerous misinformation. However, our findings of observational and experimentally controlled validity, the emergence of independent typing, and data implying validity of this technique (Calculator & Singer 1992; Cardinal Hanson & Wakeham, 1996; Heckler, 1994; Intellectual Disability Review Panel [IDRP], 1989; Karp 1993; Karp, Biklen and Chadwick 1993; Steering Committee 1993; Rimland & Green, 1993; Sheehan 1993; Sheehan and Matuozzi, 1994; Vazquez, 1994) have given us some guidelines with which to proceed.

Looking a little closer, Weiss, Wagner and Baumann's 1996 study used a design where the facilitator was out of the room; the typer was read a story as the text (multimodal of auditory and visual input) was shown on a screen and there were three separate trials. The typer answered questions correctly in 2/3 trials. Autistic children preferentially attend to synchronous audiovisual sensory input. Additionally, as children with autism are thigmotaxic, and thus particularly susceptible to influence, having the facilitator out of the room while reading the story allowed for control of *susceptibility* to influence.

Now it's important to note that while these authors changed their mind after extensive work with individuals, they close with comments and direction for future research, emphasizing the fragility of this phenomenon, which aligns with my experience. Commenting on additional case studies they were working on:

> Although these studies are not yet complete enough to report, they have contributed to our subjective impressions that this phenomenon is fragile vis-a-vis it's reliability; some days we get it (that is valid communication) and some days we do not. For example we are currently investigating facilitated communication with a young man who with his partner – facilitator, has succeeded at passing information accurately about 10 to 15% of the time. Similarly Kenny, described above in our case study, did not show valid communication in the second of our three trials. Therefore, had trial 2 been the only trial administered, we would've concluded that facilitation was not valid for communication. There are at least two hypothesis regarding the reliability of facilitated communication that we must evaluate further. It may be that facilitated communication *can* exist (is valid), but it is not always operative (that is lower reliability). Alternatively the actual validity and reliability of facilitated communication may be quite high, at least for some, but many of the experimental designs employed thus far have been unreliable in capturing the phenomenon.

But, critics were not satisfied with Weiss and colleagues study, instead accounting for the results saying the experimenter must have somehow cued the response as he was in the room when the story was read. In 2012, Mostert came out with a review of recent studies, including Weiss and Wagner's study. In his review Mostert states:

> The first problem in this study relates to subject responses facilitated by the "experimenter" in the consolidation phase. In spite of protestations to the contrary, it is highly likely that the "experimenter" was influencing the answers in this phase for several reasons. First, the experimenter was privy to the story content and, therefore, was predisposed to influence the subject's answers to story questions. The literature documented elsewhere in this review has unequivocally established that it is the facilitator rather than the subject who is responsible for answers via FC, as is probable here.

In science, when considering study design, it is always important to evaluate the impact of any particular setup. While Mostert dismisses Weiss and colleagues' findings outright because influence was shown in prior studies, he fails to consider alternative explanations, such as variations in study design.

The second study I want to review describes the process of a young boy who learned to handwrite and then type after practicing on sequentially smaller targets. After meeting Soma and learning of how she taught Tito to write, Morton Anne Gernsbacher, a cognitive psychology professor at University of Wisconsin, published a paper on a child with autism, "RH", who was able to learn to communicate by marking choices on paper with a marker. He would go on to be able to type, initially using support. Though Gernsbacher does not mention Facilitated Communication in this article, and there is no report of authorship, she describes initially needing to support RH at the hand then progressively fading the support. Part of the process she describes is similar to what RPM initially then the S2C and Spellers method propose - moving from gross motor with a marker or pencil to fine motor using his index finger to point, though also using touch support similar to FCT. The reason I suggest this case study is Gernsbacher is a cognitive psychology researcher; the parent of a nonverbal child with autism and what she describes in the case study is very similar to supported typing strategies.

Gernsbacher MA. Language is More than Speech: A Case Study. J Dev Learn Disord. 2004;8:79-96. PMID: 25520586; PMCID: PMC4266410.

The third study is a case report in chapter 6 of *Contested Words. Contested Science. Sorting It Out Under Fire: Our Journey.* This chapter describes in detail the process of one autistic typer, Eugene, taking the test that was given in the original O.D. Heck study that showed clear influence and little to no clear communication. Eugene and his support person, Mayer, found similar results in their first trial in that there was a lot of influence seen with little identification of pictures. But then they practiced on and off over the next two years and Eugene "passed" the test. By this point, though, he was independent with his typing. In describing the process, Eugene typed,

"...Please understand that facilitated communication is how I got from 'point a' to 'point b'. Readiness for independence starts from deep confidence not a 'sink or swim' mentality."

Before I close, I wanted to go back to the comment Katharine Beals made in our email exchange. She suggests that if I want to convince people of the legitimacy of FC, one way I can help is to "participate in a rigorous, videotaped message-passing experiment conducted by an independent researcher."

So, addressing the question of "why haven't the proponents done more research?" I would begin by suggesting, as detailed, supporting research *has* been done - there are case studies of independent typing and message passing; several motor learning and praxis studies; and imaging studies that align with a neurologic basis for supported typing. But at least some critics, as Beals' email to me indicates, don't seem like they will be satisfied without redoing the studies that demonstrate influence.

Beyond the actual science, the vitriolic debate has created a lack of trust on both sides. Colleagues I have known on the "proponent" side are afraid to talk about it at times for fear of getting a lot of pushback. Personally, I was told I need to "stop talking about this crap" by a well-respected professor, who I had hoped might help me. An illustrative example of the nastiness, mentioned above but worth another mention, at a recent National Institute on Deafness and Other Communication Disorders (NIDCD) web conference, with two attendees who used supported typing, one of the organizers felt the need to address social media attacks by detractors, asking for participants to be respectful and not to return to past debates:

> I am personally appalled and somewhat saddened
> about some of what is appearing in social media

related to our meeting and this sort of attack behavior will not be tolerated here.

This lack of communication and understanding between people in the debate filters down to people less familiar with this specific research so that getting funding for research becomes difficult. When I was in graduate school I was a part of a group that was applying for a grant to look into whether a mechanical device could replace physical support. Two of three reviewers rejected our proposal because "facilitated communication had been discredited."

Personally, I learned first hand that going back to graduate school in a department heavy in people doing animal research on a controversial topic is not the easiest way to succeed in academia, much less doing solid research in this area. I went into graduate school, assuming that it would not be a well received to talk about supported typing. So, attempted to keep a low profile and focused discussions more on the motor system.

But my advisor, Philip Teitelbaum, in our ten minute grilling sessions, pushed me and eventually I explained it all to him. Other than that, I never spoke at a seminar or a meeting about it, but somewhere along the way the word got out. Mentioned above, as a professor ended up telling me I needed to "stop talking about this crap". The things is, it turns out it makes it pretty challenging to study a topic you can't discuss. Changing paradigms takes a lot of work, time and money. Needless to say, it probably wasn't the smartest decision I ever made from a personal perspective - going to graduate school to get my PhD in my mid forties, so I could study a controversial subject in an animal research department. Some might say ridiculous.

That said, I hope the information in this book will allow professional organizations to fully understand *all* the research and schools and clinics will finally be more open to supporting these autistic typers - understanding that true communication happens with this method, while also understanding that influence may be part of the process as the typer works towards independence.

Definitions

Applied Behavior Analysis (ABA): ABA uses the science of behavior and learning and is used to treat autism. The idea is that if you reward a behavior, a person is likely to increase that behavior. If you ignore that behavior, it should lessen.

Early Start Denver Model (ESDM): The ESDM applies behavioral principles and knowledge of typical development to support social communication and language development.

FloorTime Therapy: Floortime is a relationship-based approach for children with autism, where the parent or therapist engages the child by joining them on the floor to play and interact.

Homunculus : A homunculus is a visual representation of the brain's motor and sensory distribution along the cerebral cortex. The size of each body part reflects the amount of cortical area dedicated to processing sensations or motor control for that part.

Ideomotor effect: An effect that happens when muscles may activate anticipating a certain action. For example, when golfers imagine making a putt, we may see activation of "putting" muscles on an EMG recording, without movement.

Institutionalization Syndrome describes changes in personality when a person is in an institution for a long period and becomes passive and dependent.

Neurodivergent: The essence of neurodivergence is a person's brain is connected differently than what is considered typical, with different strengths and challenges.

Prompt Dependency: When someone learns a skill but can't do it without someone prompting them with a verbal, visual or physical cue. Prompt dependency occurs most often in persons with autism.

Proprioception: The sense of knowing where your body is without seeing it. For example, this sense allows you to scratch an itch without looking; this sense is what allows you to know how much force to exert when picking up a fragile object without breaking it.

Rapid Prompting Method (RPM): RPM was developed by Soma Mukhopadhyay after teaching her non verbal autistic son to type and write. RPM teaches a subject then uses touch, verbal and visual prompts to access the keyboard.

Regulation: The ability to control one's thoughts and emotions so that you can participate in every day life.

Relationship Development Intervention (RDI): RDI is an autism therapy that uses amplified prompts and wait times to encourage relationships.

Social Communication Emotional Regulation Transactional Supports (SCERTS): SCERTS is an evidence-based educational framework that addresses the core domains of social communication (SC), emotional regulation (ER) by ensuring that the environment is adapted with both interpersonal and learning supports, referred to as transactional support (TS). ((Prizant, Wetherby, Rubin, Laurent & Rydell, 2006).

Sensory Integration Therapy (SIT): SIT was developed by Jean Ayres, an occupational therapist. SIT uses play therapy and sensorimotor equipment such as a platform swing or climbing structures to help a child integrate their sensory and motor system.

Thigmotaxis: according to Merriam Webster thigmotaxis is a taxis in which contact especially with a solid or rigid surface is the stimulus directing the movement of an organism with taxis being a form of movement behavior that involves movement towards or away from a stimulus.

Treatment and Education of Autistic and Communication Handicapped Children (TEACCH): is a structured teaching approach that uses visual supports, clear expectations with a structured, predictable environment.

References

Arabi, Manizheh, Alireza Saberi Kakhki, Mehdi Sohrabi, Sakineh Soltani Kouhbanani, and Mehdi Jabbari Nooghabi. 2019. "Is Visuomotor Training an Effective Intervention for Children with Autism Spectrum Disorders?" Neuropsychiatric Disease and Treatment 15 (November): 3089–3102. doi:10.2147/NDT.S214991.

Bhat, A. N. (2021). Motor impairment increases in children with autism spectrum disorder as a function of social communication, cognitive and functional impair ment, repetitive behavior.. Autism research.Janurary 2021. https://doi.org/10.1002/aur.2453

Carpenter, M. G., & Campos, J. L. (2020). The effects of hearing loss on balance: a critical review. Ear and hearing, 41, 107S-119S.

Cattaneo, L., Fabbri-Destro, M., Boria, S., Pieraccini, C., Monti, A., Cossu, G. et al. (2007). Impairment of action chains in autism and its possible role in intention understanding. *Proceedings of the National Academy of Sciences*, *104*(45), 17825-17830.

Cohen, L., & Dehaene, S. (2004). Specialization within the ventral stream: the case for the visual word form area. Neuroimage, 22(1), 466-476.

Devan, B. D., McDonald, R. J., & White, N. M. (1999). Effects of medial and lateral caudate-putamen lesions on place-and cue-guided behaviors in the water maze: relation to thigmotaxis. Behavioural brain research.

Dewey, D., Cantell, M., & Crawford, S. G. (2007). Motor and gestural performance in children with autism spectrum disorders, developmental coordination disorder, and/or attention deficit hyperactivity disorder. Journal of the International Neuropsychological Society, 13(2), 246-256.

Dunckley, V. L. (2016). Autism and screen time: Special brains, special risks. Psychology Today.

Dziuk, M. A., Larson, J. C. G., Apostu, A., Mahone, E. M., Denckla, M. B., & Mostofsky, S. H. (2007). Dyspraxia in autism: association with motor, social, and communicative deficits. Developmental Medicine & Child Neurology, 49(10), 734-739.

Fabbri-Destro, M., Cattaneo, L., Boria, S., & Rizzolatti, G. (2009). Planning actions in autism. *Experimental brain research, 192*(3), 521-525.

Filipek, P. A., Accardo, P. J., Baranek, G. T., Cook, E. H., Dawson, G., Gordon, B. et al. (2013). The Screening and Diagnosis of Autistic Spectrum Disorders1. Autism, 11-56.

Gitimoghaddam, M., Chichkine, N., McArthur, L., Sangha, S. S., & Symington, V. (2022). Applied behavior analysis in children and youth with autism spectrum disorders: a scoping review. Perspectives on behavior science, 45(3), 521-557.

Grayson, A., Emerson, A., Howard-Jones, P., & O'Neil, L. (2012). Hidden communicative competence: Case study evidence using eye- tracking and video analysis. Autism, 16(1), 75-86.

Greenwald, H. S., Knill, D. C., & Saunders, J. A. (2005). Integrating visual cues for motor control: A matter of time. Vision Research, 45(15), 1975-1989.

Hall, A. M. Et al. The influence of the therapist-patient relationship on treatment outcome in physical rehabilitation: a systematic review. Physical Therapy. (2010).

Haswell, C. C., Izawa, J., Dowell, L. R., Mostofsky, S. H., & Shadmehr, R. (2009). Representation of internal models of action in the autistic brain. Nature neuroscience, 12(8), 970-972.

Hayes, M. My Voice: One Man's Journey to Overcome the Silence of autism.vimeo.com/193191599. Retrieved 12-7-2024.

Jaswal, V. K., Lampi, A. J., & Stockwell, K. M. (2024). Literacy in nonspeaking autistic people. Autism, 13623613241230709.

Jones, A. S., & Zarcone, J. R. (2014). Comparison of prompting strategies on two types of tasks with children diagnosed with autism spectrum disorders. Behavior Analysis in Practice, 7, 51-60.

Kell, A. J. E., Koldewyn, K., & Kanwisher, N. G. (2013). The functional organization of the ventral visual pathway in adults with autism. Journal of Vision, 13(9), 832-832.

Kilroy, E., Ring, P., Hossain, A., & Nalbach…, A. (2022). Motor performance, praxis, and social skills in autism spectrum disorder and developmental coordination disorder. Autism

Kim, J. H., Yu, D. H., Huh, Y. H., Lee, E. H., Kim, H. G., & Kim, H. R. (2017). Long-term exposure to 835 MHz RF-EMF induces hyperactivity, autophagy and demyelination in the cortical neurons of mice. Scientific reports.

Klin, A., Lin, D. J., Gorrindo, P., Ramsay, G., & Jones, W. (2009). Two-year-olds with autism orient to non-social contingencies rather than biological motion. Nature, 459(7244), 257-261.

Lepping, Rebecca J., Walker S. McKinney, Grant C. Magnon, Sarah K. Keedy, Zheng Wang, Stephen A. Coombes, David E. Vaillancourt, John A. Sweeney, and Matthew W. Mosconi. "Visuomotor brain network activation and functional connectivity among individuals with autism spectrum disorder." Human brain mapping 43, no. 2 (2022): 844-859.

De Marchena, Ashley, Casey J. Zampella, Zachary Dravis, Juhi Pandey, Stewart Mostofsky, and Robert T. Schultz. "Measuring dyspraxia in autism using a five-minute praxis exam." Research in autism spectrum disorders 106 (2023): 102200.

Miller, Haylie L., Melissa K. Licari, Anjana Bhat, Lisa S. Aziz-Zadeh, Tine Van Damme, Nicholas E. Fears,

Sharon A. Cermak, and Priscila M. Tamplain. "Motor problems in autism: Co-occurrence or feature?." Developmental Medicine & Child Neurology 66, no. 1 (2024): 16-22.

Miller, M., Chukoskie, L., Zinni, M., & Townsend…, J. (2014). Miller, Michael, Leanne Chukoskie, Marla Zinni, Jeanne Townsend, and Doris Trauner. "Dyspraxia, motor function and visual–motor integration in autism." Behavioural brain research 269 (2014): 95-102.

Mottron, L., Dawson, M., Soulières, I., Hubert, B., & Burack, J. (2006). Enhanced perceptual functioning in autism: An update, and eight principles of autistic perception. Journal of autism and developmental disorders, 36, 27-43.

Müller, Ralph-Axel, Natalia Kleinhans, Nobuko Kemmotsu, Karen Pierce, and Eric Courchesne. "Abnormal variability and distribution of functional maps in autism: an FMRI study of visuomotor learning." American Journal of Psychiatry 160, no. 10 (2003): 1847-1862.

Nicoli, Giovanni, Giulia Pavon, Andrew Grayson, Anne Emerson, and Suvobrata Mitra. "Touch may reduce cognitive load during assisted typing by individuals with developmental disabilities." Frontiers in Integrative Neuroscience 17 (2023): 1181025.

Obajuluwa, Adejoke Olukayode, Ayodele Jacob Akinyemi, Olakunle Bamikole Afolabi, Khalid Adekoya, Joseph Olurotimi Sanya, and Azeez

Olakunle Ishola. "Exposure to radio-frequency electromagnetic waves alters acetylcholinesterase gene expression, exploratory and motor coordination-linked behaviour in male rats." Toxicology reports 4 (2017): 530-534.

Prizant, Barry M., Amy M. Wetherby, Emily Rubin, and Amy C. Laurent. "The SCERTS model: A transactional, family-centered approach to enhancing communication and socioemotional abilities of children with autism spectrum disorder." Infants & Young

Children 16, no. 4 (2003): 296-316.

Rawat, Seema, Somya Vats, and Praveen Kumar. "Evaluating and exploring the MYO ARMBAND." In 2016 International Conference System Modeling & Advancement in Research Trends (SMART), pp. 115-120. IEEE, 2016.

Rogers, D., Karki, C., Bartlett, C., & Pocock, P. (1991). The motor disorders of mental handicap: An overlap with the motor disorders of severe psychiatric illness. The British Journal of Psychiatry, 158(1), 97-102.

Schulz, R., Braass, H., Liuzzi, G., Hoerniss, V., & Lechner..., P. (2015). White matter integrity of premotor–motor connections is associated with motor output in chronic stroke patients. NeuroImage: Clinical.

Sharer, Elizabeth, Deana Crocetti, John Muschelli, Anita D. Barber, Mary Beth Nebel, Brian S. Caffo, Jim J. Pekar, and Stewart H.

Mostofsky. "Neural correlates of visuomotor learning in autism." Journal of child neurology 30, no. 14 (2015): 1877-1886.

Small, G. H., Brough, L. G., & Neptune, R. R. (2021). The influence of cognitive load on balance control during steady-state walking. Journal of biomechanics, 122, 110466.

Smith, I. M., & Bryson, S. E. (2007). Gesture imitation in autism: II. Symbolic gestures and pantomimed object use. Cognitive Neuropsychology, 24(7), 679-700.

Stein, D. S., Welchons, L. W., Corley, K. B., Dickinson, H., Levin, A. R., Nelson, C. A. et al. (2015). Autism associated with early institutionalization, high intelligence, and naturalistic behavior therapy in a 7-year-old boy. Journal of Developmental & Behavioral Pediatrics, 36(1), 53-55.

Torres, E. B., Brincker, M., Isenhower, R. W., Yanovich, P., Stigler, K. A., Nurnberger, J. I. et al. (2013). Autism: the micro-movement perspective. *Frontiers in integrative neuroscience, 7, 32.*

Unruh, Kathryn E., Laura E. Martin, Grant Magnon, David E. Vaillancourt, John A. Sweeney, and Matthew W. Mosconi. "Cortical and subcortical alterations associated with precision visuomotor behavior in individuals with autism spectrum disorder." Journal of neurophysiology 122, no. 4 (2019): 1330-1341.

Villalobos, M. E., Mizuno, A., Dahl, B. C., Kemmotsu, N., & Müller, R.-A. (2005). Reduced functional connectivity between V1 and inferior frontal cortex associated with visuomotor performance in autism. Neuroimage, 25(3), 916-925.

Wallis, C. (2006). Inside the autistic mind. TIME- NEW YORK- AMERICAN EDITION.

Wandell, Brian A. "The neurobiological basis of seeing words." Annals of the New York Academy of Sciences 1224, no. 1 (2011): 63-80.

Watson, A. H. D. (2006). What can studying musicians tell us about motor control of the hand. Journal of anatomy, 208(4), 527-542.

Weiss, M. J. S., Wagner, S. H., & Bauman, M. L. (1996). A validated case study of facilitated communication. Mental retardation.

Witt, S. T., Laird, A. R., & Meyerand, M. E. (2008). Functional neuroimaging correlates of finger-tapping task variations: an ALE meta-analysis. Neuroimage.

Zappullo, Isa, Massimiliano Conson, Chiara Baiano, Roberta Cecere, Gennaro Raimo, and Amanda Kirby. "The relationships between self-reported motor functioning and autistic traits: The Italian version of the adult developmental coordination disorders/ dyspraxia checklist (ADC)." International Journal of Environmental Research and Public Health 20, no. 2 (2023): 1101.

Appendix 1: The Neurology Of Typing Communication In Autism. A Summary

****This excerpt contains a fair amount of repetition from what I have laid out in the book, but in a more concise presentation.**

Aside from doing another blind trial, Beals suggested that in order to demonstrate legitimacy of FC I also need to "explain why the current account of autism as a socio-cognitive disorder that undermines language (and literacy) acquisition is wrong and to provide an alternative account of autism spectrum disorders that does a better job accounting for all the data on autism, across the autism spectrum, and that makes better scientific predictions, across the autism spectrum. (A tall order, I recognize, given that the socio-cognitive take on autism has been accumulating massive amounts of corroborating research for about 8 decades)".

The weird thing is I think several scientists have been doing just that. Beals talks about autism being a sociocognitive disorder, but most scientists now believe that autism is a neurobiological disorder in that brain connections connect differently during development. But that doesn't mean autism isn't a sociocognitive disorder as well as a neurobiological disorder. What Beals doesn't seem to evidence understanding of is that brain connections *underlie* sociocognitive functions.

When I was first considering how to study supported typing I believed that we would have to address why there was so much influence in those original studies. How could my experience with Kris have been so different than what I saw in those studies? Kris would push the board away from me in protest until the time he had some thing he really needed to say. The way he pushed against my hand towards the board when he typed RAFFI was discordant with the image I had of individuals sitting for an extended test, subtly letting themselves be influenced.

The second thing I thought we would need to account for is how someone could pick up on the written word without being taught. In this book I reference that the bottom part of the visual pathways, the ventral stream, has been show to be efficiently connected in autism. Why does this matter? Well, for one, researchers have a strong theory of how the brain processes whole word reading, and that involves the ventral occipital temporal area of the cerebral cortex - a brain connection that appears well developed in autism.

Wandell, B. A. (2011). The neurobiological basis of seeing words.

Annals of the New York Academy of Sciences.

The third thing I considered was how to demonstrate communication from the typer while controlling for the influence. This one was hard as I knew Kris typed with me, but the fragility of his typing communication, as Weiss and colleagues put it, didn't allow for an experimental set up as was done in the O. D. Heck study. Examining the studies that do evidence clear message passing, the protocol called for the support people, or facilitators to be out of the room. While a story was being read, rather than using visual and/or auditory blocks, the support person was out of the room. Further, these studies did not have a trial where the facilitator sees one thing, but the typer sees something different, something a lot of detractors ask for in a double blind trial. While it's informative to know that when two different pictures are shown what is typed many times is what the facilitator sees, we already know this. We know that there can be influence. What has been shown is that when protocols don't include visual and auditory blinders, we are much less likely to see influence. Whereas if you use these blinders *and* set up conditions where the typer and the support person are seeing different things, we are *optimizing* the potential for influence through the ideomotor effect and <u>thigmotaxis</u>.

Minshew NJ, Williams DL. The new neurobiology of autism: cortex, connectivity, and neuronal organization. Arch Neurol. 2007 Jul;64(7:945-50. doi: 10.1001/ archneur.64.7.945. Erratum in: Arch Neurol. 2007 Oct;64(10:1464. PMID: 17620483; PMCID: PMC2597785.

To understand the neurologic basis underlying supported typing, let's turn to three of the primary supports that have been used in supported typing. 1 Amplified proprioception through resistance or touch; 2 Handing someone a marker or pen to initiate a movement 3 Rhythm through encouraging words or metronome.

Amplified Proprioception

If we compare what we know about the autistic nervous system, to what we know from autobiographical accounts, to what we know about the communication supports used, we can start to find a neurologic rationale. Let's start with amplified proprioception. Facilitated Communication recommends going from a least to most strategy of support. That is, if someone can type on a keyboard without support, then no support is needed. On the other end of the support here, you may need to support the index finger and push back as the person goes forward to the keyboard. Shoulder and elbow support would be inbetween. So why would someone need resistance to control movements? One theory I have is that the neural connections that connect the main sensory part of the brain (primary sensory cortex) to the main motor area of the brain (primary motor cortex) are "over connected" in the autistic brain - conceivably more accessible. These connections then connect to different areas in the frontal lobe, higher order motor areas. At the same time, the maps, or homunculi we have in our brains, thought to be responsible for body awareness, are not developed well. Let's reflect on a quote from Chandima Rajapatirana, a FC user:

> ..Helplessly I sit while Mom calls me to come. I know what I must do, but often I can't get up until she says, 'Stand up,'" he writes. "[The] knack of knowing where my body is does not come easy for me. Interestingly I do not know if I am sitting or standing. I am not aware of my body unless it is touching something … Your hand on mine lets me know

where my hand is. Jarring my legs by walking tells me I am alive.

Wallis, C. (200. Inside the autistic mind. *TIME-NEW YORK-AMERICAN EDITION.*

Explaining further: If you have a hard time feeling and controlling your body, but as Chammi says, you don't feel it unless you move—why would that be? One possible explanation is that the U loops are connected well between the main sensory and motor areas. These connections are then connected to the next "U loop" to the higher motor areas in the brain. Thus, by actively using muscles, it is plausible you are also connecting higher motor areas and thus gain more motor control. When someone has had a stroke and loses motor output, if these U loop connections are left intact, the better the residual motor output. In other words if the U loops aren't affected by the stroke, the person does better on motor tasks. It is conceivable that similarly, autistic persons affected by dyspraxia can similarly "take advantage" of these connections to access the motor system.

Schulz, R., Braass, H., Liuzzi, G., Hoerniss, V., & Lechner..., P. (2015). White matter integrity of premotor–motor connections is associated with motor output in chronic stroke patients. *NeuroImage: Clinical.*

Pencil to initiate movement

The Rapid Prompting Method (RPM), Spelling to Communicate (S2C) and the Spellers Method all recommend using a pencil or marker to have the child push towards a stencil of gradually smaller sizes, as they improve with motor control.

The emphasis is on using educational lessons to work on typing accuracy. Soma, the woman who created RPM, says handing the pencil is "the prompt". From a neurological perspective, I see three possibilities: 1) Handing the pencil requires the person to activate muscles, thereby accessing the U loops; 2) As autistic individuals tend to associate movement with meaning derived from objects (see Smith & Bryson), the pencil may serve as an external cue for them to initiate movement; and 3) Communication partners using this method routinely combine handing the pencil with a verbal prompt, such as "The first letter is...," delivered in a rhythmic pattern. Handing the pencil may support motor initiation through rhythm as well.

Rhythm

There's a specialty in music therapy called neurologic music therapy (NMT[©]). NMT has looked at how rhythm supports movement. One study that investigated the timing of movements showed that if you were to go in an imaging machine and tap your fingers to a metronome, you would only "require" the primary motor cortex to be active. On the other hand if you were to try tapping your fingers to a beat, but had no external rhythm cue, so had to internalize the timing, you would see higher level motor areas active. So, rhythm is a way to support access to the motor system by providing a scaffold to the primary motor area.

Witt, S. T., Laird, A. R., & Meyerand, M. E. (2008). Functional neuroimaging correlates of finger-tapping task variations: an ALE meta-analysis. *Neuroimage.*

Appendix 2: Summary And Thoughts On The Different Supported Typing Strategies

Rehabilitation scientists suggest focusing on the key ingredients of benefits from particular therapies, rather than a "package". For example, when doing therapy with a person with stroke, is it the aerobic exercise or strengthening that impacts recovery best? I suggest that the supports used of rhythm, amplified proprioception or the pencil cue are some of the "key ingredients" used in supported typing strategies. I have addressed why these supports work from a neurologic perspective, but I don't think we know yet what strategy is optimal for different challenges the typer presents with.

Gotor learning difficulties. Generally, autistic individuals also have similar differences in terms of brain connectivity, so, generally, the supports used in supported typing would be applicable. But, there *are* differences in terms of how easy eye movements are or aren't for a given individual. There are differences in terms of how regulated or dysregulated an individual is. There are differences in terms of the level of dyspraxia or visuomotor challenges.

Parents have asked me what supported typing method works best. My common reply is it is all one brain, and elements of each method could support a particular challenge better. For example, if a child has difficulty with voluntary eye movements, common in autism, a keyboard with contrasting colors may be more supportive - maybe combined with some visuomotor exercises. Eye hand coordination is another thing to consider. I have known children who have such poor eye hand coordination that they have trouble reaching out to a door knob. If a child has severe eye hand coordination difficulties (the visuomotor system, then he may benefit from more amplified proprioception as I have observed the resistance helps to bring the eyes in.

As such, I recommend working together with a good therapist to see what particular challenges a person has and what supports work best.

Appendix 3: A Note About Criticisms Of ABA From The Author

I address many of the downsides of Applied Behavior Analysis (ABA in this book - in fact am fairly critical. This is a result of my professional experience of over 30 years of serving people with autism; speaking with parents and therapists; and studying the ABA method. Though I do mention the ways I have observed how ABA methods can be useful, in my years of experience. I have seen many downsides. All that said, I need to acknowledge that I know there are many hardworking people working within the system to make a change, Inappropriate Possum for one.

There are many treatment "packages" in autism therapies. **Floortime**, ABA, the Treatment and Education of Autistic and Communication Handicapped Children **TEACCH, The Early Start Denver Model** (ESDM, **Relationship Development Intervention** (RDI, the **Social Communication, Emotional Regulation, and Transactional Support** (SCERTS to name a few. Many of these therapies have overlap in terms of the "key ingredients", but few incorporate what we know about autistic neurological differences. The reason I focus on ABA is ABA has been marketed as the "gold standard" of autism treatment, and this recognition paralleled the time when supported typing was "discovered". It is also important to note that if one wants to become an autism specialist, the training is heavily weighted to learning the behavioral strategies of ABA. This is also the case if one wants to become a special educator. Whereas supported typing advocates believe that dyspraxia is foundational in understanding nonverbal autism, ABA professionals believe intellectual impairment describes nonverbal autism best.

I use the word marketed, above, in that while there is science supporting ABA, that science  has been questioned and I believe that marketing and financial reward also plays a not inconsequential role. Jaime Hoerricks, PHDA takes a close look at the process of how finances - including insurance coverage, funding resources, government resources and promotion by autism agencies contributed to an ingrained "ABA-first" approach.

All that said, some components of behavior analysis are important in *any* therapy session. ABA rewards successes. ABA ignores negative behavior. ABA provides a structure for how to manage behavior that is not working well for a child or family. For example, ABA principles look for a replacement behavior for a behavior that isn't working well for a child or her family. But, what ABA specialists do *not* do is consider the underlying neurology. Let's take an example of an autistic person who is a "runner" - they run away and aren't aware of safety concerns.

This is obviously a safety concern. If you look at it as an ABA therapist you might determine that this is "non compliance" or "escape" behavior, so this therapist would set up a plan working towards having the child not run away using reinforcements such as a candy the child likes.

But, if a therapist incorporates what we know from autobiographical accounts and scientific studies, she would understand that actively using muscles increases body awareness, so this child might be craving movement or deep pressure. Using supports to increase movement time or increased deep pressure along with other sensory supports can support the child with their unique neurological differences.

By describing running away as "non compliance" or "escape" behavior, the therapist is assigning meaning to the running away behavior - they are assuming the child is running away to get away from something they don't want to do. By using known neurological differences to try and understand behavior, it allows a therapist to address the behavior with supports that address these *neurological* differences, rather than ascribing the function in a negative way. Instead of suggesting the child is trying to escape from something they don't want, there is an understanding of what they *need*, based on their different brain connectivity - so using amplified proprioception in a variety of ways can help the child with body awareness so there is less of a need to run or move.

On the negativity I have felt when interacting with ABA professionals, in almost 40 years of working with children and adults with autism, I have consulted a fair amount with other speech occupational and physical therapists. I have had little difficulty collaborating with these professionals. On the other hand, I have found a lot of difficulty collaborating with ABA therapists, and instead have largely experienced disrespect and "ignoring" behavior. Another blog post illustrates this (<u>ABA Myth</u>).

Lastly, I want to emphasize that if people want to become autism specialists, the curriculum currently is weighted to learning ABA methods. I think we can do better.

Rehabilitation scientists talk about the "key ingredients" of therapies, rather than a particular treatment package. I firmly believe that autism therapy key ingredients could be greatly enhanced if There were collaborative discussions between *all* professionals, and 2) ABA professionals were trained in autistic neurology.

Glossary for QR codes

1. Documentary of Matt, a typer who learns to speak with typing.
https://vimeo.193191599

2. Video excerpt of typer communicating frustration over constant questioning of what is typed.
https://unitedforcommunicationchoice.org/grant-blasko-no-puppet-strings/846/

3. Video of professor detailing Facilitated Communication.
https://www.youtube.com/watch?v=1j0TAaDWrxU&t=2898s

4. Ido YouTube video.
https://www.youtube.com/watch?v=oNlLez0bGbc

5. Tito on 60 Minutes
https://www.youtube.com/watch?v=Nfiap3a7Tuo

6. Tito and Ralph Savarese
https://www.youtube.com/watch?v=PamjosXYiKo&t=2906s

7. Criticism of Tito on 60 minutes
https://www.fhijournal.org/20-6/

8. An article criticizing ABA
https://autside.substack.com/p/the-aba-myth-unmasking-americas-autism

9. An article demonstrating PTSD related to ABA. https://www.emerald.com/insight/content/doi/10.1108/aia-08-2017-0016/full/html

10.   Rothenberg shock video https://www.youtube.com/watch?v=YcxpGKctZMs151

11.   Blog post on the Rotenberg Center https://www.youtube.com/watch?v=YcxpGKctZMs

12.   The motor cortex https://en.wikipedia.org/wiki/Motor_cortex

13.   Video comparing movement of typical vs autistic child https://vimeo.com/644170273

14.   Autism is a World Documentary https://www.youtube.com/watch?v=U1wsiVYCqn0

15.   Beal on autism is a world https://www.facilitatedcommunication.org/blog/autism-is-a-world-is-a-world

16.   Paper on SMA to PMA connectivity. https://pubmed.ncbi.nlm.nih.gov/22623093/

17.   See # 8

About Kris' Camp